THE ELEMENTS OF CRITICAL READING

John Peters

CALIFORNIA STATE UNIVERSITY, NORTHRIDGE

D0980911

DISCARD

ALLYN AND BACON
BOSTON · LONDON · TORONTO · SYDNEY · TOKYO · SINGAPORE

Copyright © 1991 by Allyn & Bacon
A Viacom Company
Needham Heights, Massachusetts 02194

Internet: www.abacon.com
America Online: keyword: College Online

All rights reserved. No part of the material
protected by this copyright may be reproduced or
utilized in any form or by any means, electronic
or mechanical, including photocopying,
recording, or by any information storage and
retrieval system, without the written permission
of the copyright owner.

ISBN 0-02-394601-6
Printed in the United States of America
10 9 8 7 6 5   00 99 98 97

The following have granted permission to reprint material on:

Page 6: From *The Sea Around Us*, Revised   Edition, by
Rachel L. Carson. Copyright 1950, 1951, 1961 by Rachel L.
Carson; renewed by Roger Christie. Reprinted by permission
of Oxford University Press, Inc.

Page 6: From Marjorie L. Zeff, "Sedimentation in a Salt
Marsh-Tidal Channel System, Southern New Jersey," *Marine
Geology* 82 (1988): 33-48. Copyright © 1988 by Elsevier
Science Publishers B.V. Reprinted by permission of the
publishers and author.

continued on page 179

Preface

This is a book about reading and elementary criticism. It is addressed to college undergraduates who must learn traditional ways of analyzing, discussing, and evaluating what they are assigned to read. In a wider sense, however, this book is for anyone—in college or out—who must read often and who is in some doubt as to what "critical reading" means.

Obviously a text of this length, intended for a general audience and informally structured, cannot boast of how thoroughly it covers the finer points of criticism. Nor can it claim to represent the sectarian interests of each and every school of critical theory. Our approach in this case must be general. But nowadays when academic specialization and sophisticated methodology soon challenge anyone pursuing college-level studies, a reader needs to recognize the most general and widely relevant procedures early on. For that reason, this book is really less about rules to follow than about directions to take. It is about possibilities for looking further at a text of any kind. My purpose has been merely to define, to illustrate, and to suggest. The rest depends on the individual reader, who of course will respond personally to each text he or she reads.

I wish to thank several students of mine whose papers I have quoted: Julie Adamson, Manuel Gonzales, Jamie Jobe, Peter McDonald, Mary Jane Quinn, and Brian Wilson. For

FEB - 1999

production assistance, I am grateful to Barbara Zeiders, Betsy Keefer, and Aliza Greenblatt. Finally, for his guidance and patience, I owe special gratitude to my editor at Macmillan, D. Anthony English.

                                                    J.P.

Contents

PART ONE

Reading

Chapter 1

Reading Across the Disciplines

To be a critical reader you first need something to read. Let's consider for a moment how vast the possibilities are. An average public library contains a few thousand volumes. A large college library might hold 1 or 2 million. The U.S. Library of Congress in Washington houses more than 20 million volumes, every page of which you have a Constitutional right to read. Beyond that there is all the material that libraries do not normally collect — advertising, memoranda, questionnaires, user manuals, and ordinary correspondence. The U.S. Postal Service delivers more than 160 billion pieces of mail each year, enough to keep us all busy.

In other words, the amount of material out there waiting to be read is overwhelming. Each of us has time for only a fraction of what is available, and it is unlikely that any two of us will ever read exactly the same number and variety of things. That fact makes it hard to generalize about what reading means, for as readers we do not often share the same experiences.

But we can think of reading as a general process if we keep in mind a few key terms which apply to all kinds of reading. Let's begin this book by reviewing some of those important terms.

What Is a Text?

The word *text* (from the Latin *texere*, to weave) refers to the words and form of a written work. Modern critical theory now applies that word to all kinds of writing, not just textbooks or official documents. A text can be an essay, a book, a letter, an advertisement, or even a restaurant menu. Because it has such wide relevance, *text* is a very useful word in any discussion of reading. For no matter what you've read, the material you are discussing can be called "the text."

Which texts you read may depend on such factors as the courses you take, the career you choose, the personal interests you wish to pursue, or whatever you find on the nearest coffee table. But you can expect that the range of texts you encounter during your lifetime will be enormous. Furthermore, you can be sure that the kinds of texts you read will acquaint you with a large number of disciplines.

What Is a Discipline?

Discipline has to do with orderly conduct in the pursuit of knowledge. In college we use the term to refer to a field of study. Thus biology, history, economics, psychology, engineering, and all the other majors that a student might choose are called "disciplines." Beyond college those same disciplines continue as professions. As we know, every profession generates plenty of texts about itself.

Each text is likely to reflect a discipline in which the author has specialized. Most nonfiction is written by specialists representing their own fields. We expect articles on medicine to be written by qualified doctors, financial columns to be the work of economists, and so on. Nowadays specialization even applies in the case of imaginative works such as drama and fiction. So even though there is such a thing as reading to "escape" from our everyday problems, there is no escaping the disciplines that lie behind what there is to read.

What Does "Reading Across Disciplines" Mean?

In one sense "reading across disciplines" means reading widely — not limiting yourself to one subject or field of study. To some degree that sort of reading is an inevitable part of everyday life. If you check the vitamin listings on a cereal box, study a map on the way to a meeting, browse through the direct-mail advertising you receive, or scan the evening paper — you're reading across disciplines that include health science, cartography, marketing research, and journalism. Who can avoid reading across disciplines in this ordinary way?

But in another sense, reading across disciplines means *studying* what's going on in areas outside your own major field of interest. Reading in this way requires an active commitment on your part to become informed about developments in many separate fields. Investigating those developments is very much a part of higher education. That is why college undergraduates are required to take courses in several fields as part of their general education. If your passion is biology or economics but you take time to study history, philosophy, and art as well, you're crossing the border between your chosen discipline and those of your colleagues. Those border crossings can increase your awareness of the world and make you a better educated person.

Reading across disciplines in this committed way can be difficult, however, because there are language barriers even when the language remains your own. Sooner or later you'll run up against the problem of "audience level."

What Is Audience Level?

Audience level has to do with how much previous knowledge someone needs in order to read a given text easily. Such previous knowledge may include special vocabulary, little-known facts, certain kinds of personal experience, or even prerequisite reading in the subject. The more previous knowledge a text expects of you, the "higher" the audience level; the less it requires of you, the "lower" — or more "general" — the audience level.

For example, consider the following passage from Rachel Carson's *The Sea Around Us*, a popular book written for general audiences:

> The tides are a response of the mobile waters of the ocean to the pull of the moon and the more distant sun. In theory, there is a gravitational attraction between every drop of sea water and even the outermost star of the universe. In practice, however, the pull of the remote stars is so slight as to be obliterated in the vaster movements by which the ocean yields to the moon and the sun. Anyone who has lived near tidewater knows that the moon, far more than the sun, controls the tides.

Smooth, isn't it? You probably had little or no difficulty following the author's terms and syntax. After all, she wrote the book for general readers and not exclusively for experts in her field. But now consider another passage. This one is from a scholarly article written by Marjorie L. Zeff, a marine geologist who is addressing an audience of experts:

> Previous studies of tidal marsh channels have been limited in scope. For instance, Pestrong (1965) restricted at-a-station hydraulic geometry measurements to a single channel cross section within a complex system. Barwis (1978) was concerned with point bar geometry and deposits of one channel in two South Carolina marshes and Ward (1981) investigated suspended sediment transport in one channel cross section. This present study uniquely characterizes tidal channel sedimentary processes by integrating several different aspects (morphometry, modern processes and depositional facies) of each of the channel types that make up a salt marsh system.

> — from "Sedimentation in a Salt Marsh-Tidal Channel System, Southern New Jersey," *Marine Geology* 82 (1988): 33–48

If you happen to be a specialist in marine geology, this passage may have been smooth sailing. But if you do not have much previous knowledge of the field, such terms as "at-a-station hydraulic geometry" and "suspended sediment transport" could make for troubled waters. You might need help from reference books or professors to keep your reading comprehension afloat.

One problem with reading across disciplines is that we can't always predict the audience levels of the texts we encounter. Some books will be harder to read than others. That troublesome fact forces everyone to keep estimating his or her own audience level with respect to each new text.

How Can You Estimate Your Audience Level with Respect to a Text?

The simplest way to tell where you stand in relation to a given text is to discover how much help you need to follow its vocabulary. The greater the gap between your previous knowledge and what the author expects of his or her audience, the more help you may need.

Let's take two simple examples. Suppose that you're faced with trying to read a document written in a foreign language you've never studied. In this case, your audience level will be close to "zero" because you'll need to look up almost every word in a bilingual dictionary or find a translator. On the other hand, suppose you're reading a letter from a relative who alludes often to people and places you're familiar with: "Bill and Linda are going to the lake to spend Memorial Day with Aunt Margie." As the writer's relative, you'll already know who Bill and Linda are, which lake is being referred to, and so on. Your audience level in this case is going to be much higher than that of any reader who couldn't recognize the names and places mentioned by the writer.

Most of what you read will fall somewhere between those two extremes. Chances are that your audience level will not often be zero, no matter how technically complicated the material. But you'll be facing plenty of books, articles, and documents that are less readily understood than a letter from home. Your audience level will vary from text to text. To realize where you stand in relation to each, you should be honest about how much of the text calls for previous knowledge you haven't yet acquired.

When Is Reading Above Your Audience Level Necessary or Desirable?

The answer is that it is often necessary and often desirable. Because none of us is an expert in every subject area, we are bound to face plenty of "difficult" material as we read across disciplines. Examples include voter pamphlets, legal contracts, operations manuals, as well as textbooks and business reports. But facing such material is a necessary part of our lives in a technological society.

Although many authors try to write for "general audiences" in order to keep from going over the reader's head, there is no way to guarantee mass understanding. As the critic Walter J. Ong has said, the writer's audience is always a "fiction." In other words, the writer imagines an ideal reader who will share his or her previous knowledge. But, of course, there are no ideal readers — there are only real ones. Because each of us has different kinds of previous knowledge, each of us will have different problems as we face different texts. But that is not necessarily a bad thing.

Reading hard material can be desirable because we are forced to look things up, puzzle out passages, ask questions, and thus engage actively in broadening our awareness. If we insisted on reading only what was easy for us, we would be missing the challenge of higher education.

How Can Reading Across Disciplines Improve Your Education?

Keep in mind that education is not just a process of limiting yourself to one special area of knowledge. We all need to become experts when it comes to our careers. But if the pressures of specialization box us in too tightly, we'll suffer from ignorance no matter how learned we think we are. The real object of education, said the philosopher Herbert Spencer, is "the formation of character." If we want to be whole human beings with minds of our own, we can't set out to package ourselves like appliances — each with its special function but otherwise useless.

Reading across disciplines is part of what makes social communication possible. It is what allows the scientist to talk with the artist or the business executive to trade ideas with the teacher. It is what helps us make contact with others across a world of ideas. Therefore, we should welcome the chance to read things from fields that are not our own. Even if the texts are sometimes difficult, they can widen our horizons and help us live with each other.

What Skills Are Needed for Reading Across Disciplines?

Many people think that "reading skills" are simply the basic tools of comprehension. But there is more to reading across disciplines than that. Obviously, if you're going to be doing a great deal of reading, it helps to be able to read at different speeds, to recognize main points, and to remember the essential content of the material. Those basic skills are ones you should have mastered before high school graduation, for they are necessary to any program of adult learning. But beyond the basic skills there are others to acquire, and it is with those more advanced skills that this book is mainly concerned. It's not enough just to "know how to read" if you are facing a wide variety of texts from across disciplines. You need to become skilled at analyzing and evaluating written material. In other words, you need to practice critical reading.

What Is Critical Reading?

In general, we might define *critical reading* as the act of criticism applied to the act of reading. Criticism (a word derived from the Greek *krinein*, to discern) is in turn defined by one dictionary as "analysis of qualities and evaluation of comparative worth." Thus we might say that in simple terms critical reading means analyzing and evaluating what we read.

Once we take up the issue of *how* the analyzing and evaluating are to be carried out, however, we soon discover that in practice critical reading means different things to different people. To some, it means being on the lookout for falsehoods or logical inconsistencies. To others, it means judging a text according to certain preconceived standards of quality or excellence. Still others see critical reading as the act of interpreting the text's messages or "codes" of meaning. And there are those who see critical reading as comparative reading — that is, the act of noting similarities and differences between one text and another or between one part of a text and another part of the same text. We could go on.

Let us say that critical reading allows for all of those possible definitions and more. What, then, do they all have in common? What can we detect as the thread running through these varied notions of what critical reading means? The answer we are led to is simply this: What critical reading means exactly will depend a great deal on who is doing the reading. In other words, different people bring different interests to bear on what they read, and thus their ways of criticizing also differ, according to their separate views. Ultimately, then, critical reading must be a process of *personal response*.

Why Does Personal Response Matter in Critical Reading?

By recognizing that critical reading is a process of personal response, we can also begin to see why any general definition of the term must provide for different points of view on any text. To put it another way, critical reading has to be seen as a *perspectival* activity. That is, it must be an activity whose outcome depends on the perspective or perspectives that a given reader works from when analyzing and evaluating a text. In Part II of this book, we examine in detail what some of those possible perspectives are.

But even though critical reading must be "perspectival" in the sense of allowing many points of view on a text, it remains a *process* which can be described as having a few main stages. Those stages seem common to all methods of critical reading, no matter which points of view you may favor in analyzing and evaluating what you read.

What Are the Stages of Critical Reading?

This book focuses on critical reading as a response process with four stages. Those stages correspond to the normal activities required of college students who are assigned to study texts from across the disciplines: (1) *reading* for comprehension; (2) *interpreting* the text; (3) *judging* or evaluating the text; and (4) *writing* about what you've read.

Of these four stages, the first corresponds to what people often think of as "reading." Obviously, the need to comprehend and remember what you've read is basic to any reading experience. There are, however, as we'll see in the next chapter, various habits that can help to improve that basic comprehension, especially in the case of texts that aim at a high audience level.

The second stage — interpreting — is where things start to become "critical." To interpret is to choose ways of looking back at what you've read in order to reveal its significance for you. Here we shall consider how a text can be viewed from social, emotional, rhetorical, logical, and ethical perspectives.

The third stage — judging — is a result of the interpreting process. Here we shall be concerned with how you as a critic can apply personal values in making up your mind about the overall qualities of a text.

Finally, the fourth stage — writing — brings together the three earlier stages in a creative activity of your own. Writing about what you've read is a way of showing yourself as

well as others what you really think. It is through writing
that the process of critical reading becomes complete.

Summary

This opening chapter has reviewed some key terms having
to do with reading as an activity. Remember that a "text"
can be anything you read, that "reading across disciplines"
calls for active interest in a variety of fields, and that "audience level" is one challenge every reader faces. We have
defined critical reading as a process of personal response. It
is also a "perspectival" activity that depends on each reader's
viewpoint. This book will discuss four stages of the critical
process: reading, interpreting, judging, and writing.

Chapter 2

Elementary Rules of Reading

This chapter is about reading in general. No matter what you read, some habits can make the experience more rewarding than it otherwise might be. The following rules specify what those habits are.

Examine Organizational Features

When you first encounter a text of any kind, you should pause to examine its outward features. Depending on the kind of text, those may include cover, title page, table of contents, chapter or section divisions, glossary, notes, bibliography, and other accessories. Together they will give you a first impression that may prove useful as a guide to the rest.

Remember, of course, that a text is *not* its outward features. You should never assume too much from what you see at first glance. Any *cover*—be it a dust jacket on a book or the cover photo on a magazine—will try to charm you. But covers are designed by artists who are sometimes more talented than the authors they serve. And even though we expect a *title* to relate clearly to the text it introduces, some titles have proven misleading to naive readers. *The Divine Comedy*, for example, is not a work of humor.

In the case of nonfiction books, the most useful outward features are likely to be the title page, the table of contents, and the index. The title page will give you the title, the author, and the publisher, as well as the book's date (often on the back of the title page). The table of contents gives you a sort of road map of the whole book, showing you at a glance how everything is organized and what main items of interest you'll be finding as you travel from beginning to end. The index lists topics alphabetically to help you discover whether a matter you want to know about is discussed by the author.

It's also wise to examine other features that appear at the end of a long text. You may find a glossary that defines obscure terms, an appendix that clarifies sources, and/or a bibliography that lists useful references. Few texts contain all such addenda, but those that do will have provided lavish amenities that only a fool would ignore.

Know When the Text Was Written

There are good reasons for checking to see when a text was written. If you are reading a scientific report, the findings may be out of date owing to more recent research. Or, if you're reading an essay written dozens or hundreds of years ago, the allusions to persons and events may be hard to understand without help from reference books. Forming a good relationship with an older text depends on your knowing something about the world of that text's origins.

The farther back in time we travel, the more language becomes obscure to a reader who lacks historical awareness. If we visit E. M. Forster's famous essay "What I Believe," for example, we may wonder what the author means when he says "these are strenuous and serious days, and one likes to say what one thinks while speech is comparatively free: it may not be free much longer." Only the text's date (1939) makes us realize that the author was expecting the outbreak of World War II. Or, if we happen to be reading Mary Wollstonecraft's angry diatribe against the slavish dependence of her sex, it is useful to know that *A Vindication of the Rights of Woman* is dated 1792, and to know also a bit about the history of eighteenth-century Europe.

We can't make ourselves into historians every time we pick up something to read. But we can at least check first-publication dates as well as any editors' notes that may tell us when the manuscript was completed. We can keep reference books handy, try to learn something about the author's life and times, and be ready to travel long distances in the history of ideas.

Determine Apparent Aims

Once you've examined outward features and discovered the date, it will be time to introduce yourself to the text by reading selected parts. Popular terms for this procedure include "pre-reading" and "x-raying." A simpler term might be "spot reading." The objective is to inspect parts which can give you an idea of the text's aims and audience level.

Spot reading should usually begin at the beginning. You might read the preface, if there is one, and/or the first few paragraphs of the first chapter, for it is up front that the main signals are often given. You want to know whether the writing seems easy or hard to comprehend, whether it is directed to a general readership or to specialists, and whether or not you will need reference books to assist you. From the first few pages you should get a sense of the author's style, the tone of voice, and the general dimensions of the topic or theme.

Which other parts you choose to spot read may depend on what kind of text you're dealing with. If it is a nonfictional work, the quickest way to see where it all leads might be to go straight to the end. A lucid conclusion that summarizes the text's main points and restates key aims may be as effective as a preface in letting you know what to expect if you go back and read the whole thing. Whether or not the text has a formal conclusion, it's also advisable to do a bit of drifting back and forth through the center, eyeing those spots where expository writing often focuses its aims. Those spots might include the following: (1) the first paragraph; (2) the first sentence of each body paragraph; (3) the concluding paragraph of each chapter or section; and (4) any visual aids, such as charts or graphs. Those spots can give you clues to the overall structure and content of the writing. But of course they will only give you a rough idea of the whole text.

Works of imaginative literature are often more difficult than nonfiction to "spot read." In the case of novels and short stories, there is no real advantage in skipping ahead to the end or attempting to figure out the apparent aims by selective glimpsing. There will probably be too many plot and suspense devices to permit such easy access. Besides, you deny yourself the pleasure of discovery if you try to find the plot's outcome in advance. Instead, the best approach to spot reading an imaginative work is to begin at the beginning and read on until you have a feel for the world of the text. Some would say that is also the best way to approach nonfiction, too, provided that you have the time.

Adapt to the Genre

Different types of writing call for different kinds of reading. Just as a traveler must adjust to the climates and customs of distant places, so the reader must learn to adapt to a range of textual environments. There are time-honored distinctions among *genres* (French for "types"). It is wise to respect the forms, customs, and manners of the traditional types of literature.

Much of what you read will be *nonfiction*, meaning texts that convey factual information. This genre includes many subgenres, such as the essay, textbook, business report, biography, and so on. From nonfiction you should usually expect an orderly discussion such as you might hear at a lecture or business meeting. It's a good idea to approach nonfictional texts with an open but slightly skeptical mind, remembering that some of them may contain misinformation and that others may raise more questions than they answer. In general, your relation to nonfiction is that of a student, colleague, or general reader who wants information upon which to base opinions, decisions, or future activity related to the subject.

The genres of *imaginative literature* include fiction, poetry, and drama. Though works in these categories may also be based on real events or actual problems, here the author's imagination takes precedence. There is a freedom or "poetic license" which excuses the text from ordinary standards of proof. Reading such works well takes patience because they tend to be elusive in what they have to say. To relate sympathetically to novels, short stories, poems, and plays, you must be prepared for suspense, digression, symbolism, and other subtle devices of the storyteller's art. You mustn't expect from them the same sort of businesslike presentation that you normally get from nonfiction.

Listen to the Language

Readers sometimes disregard the emotions of a text. If your only purpose is to find the message of the lesson or the solution to the plot, you may miss the silent music that language is capable of. Also, you may misread the author's voice, hearing only a dull monotone where there is quiet sentiment, or mere mumbling where there is laughter between the lines. Careful reading calls for attention to how the text sounds.

In reality, of course, the text has no "voice." The only medium is visual, though the illusion of sound is created in the reader's mind. Much of this process has to do with the cadences and rhythms of the prose. A series of short, breathy sentences can sound nervous. But if the lines are long rolling waves of words, as at the climax of a speech, the voice can be full of thunder and lightning:

When my eyes shall be turned to behold for the last time the sun in heaven, may I not see him shining on the broken

and dishonored fragments of a once glorious Union; on
States dissevered, discordant, belligerent; on a land rent with
civil feuds, or drenched, it may be, in fraternal blood.

— Daniel Webster, Speech (26 Jan. 1830)

Or, if the sentence lengths vary widely and the pace becomes uneven, you may be hearing the conversational tone
of someone sitting near you:

"Your grandmother says you read a lot. Every chance you
get. That's good, but not good enough. Words mean more
than what is set down on paper. It takes the human voice to
infuse them with the shades of deeper meaning."

I memorized the part about the human voice infusing
words. It seemed so valid and poetic.

She said she was going to give me some books and that I
not only must read them, I must read them aloud. She
suggested that I try to make a sentence sound in as many
different ways as possible.

"I'll accept no excuse if you return a book to me that has
been badly handled." My imagination boggled at the punish-
ment I would deserve if in fact I did abuse a book of Mrs.
Flowers'. Death would be too kind and brief.

— Maya Angelou, *I Know Why
the Caged Bird Sings* (1969)

Then again, if the sentences are of fairly even length and
marked by few comma breaks, you may be reading what is
often called "textbook prose." Here the author's tone is
neither bombastic nor quietly confidential, but serious and
somewhat reserved:

As philosopher of science Karl Popper has emphasized, a
good theory is characterized by the fact that it makes a
number of predictions that could in principle be disproved
or falsified by observation. Each time new experiments are
observed to agree with the predictions the theory survives,
and our confidence in it is increased; but if ever a new observation is found to disagree, we have to abandon or modify
the theory. At least that is what is supposed to happen, but

you can always question the competence of the person who carried out the observation.

> — Stephen W. Hawking,
> *A Brief History of Time* (1988)

Sentence rhythm thus lends itself to different purposes and results in different tones. It is worth noting, however, that many of the most memorable prose styles in English are slightly eccentric. That is, they do not always follow the conventional tendency to match the type of content to the type of rhythm associated with that content. Humor, for example, often depends on a writer's turning an elevated prose rhythm to ironic purposes:

> More than any other time in history, mankind faces a cross-roads. One path leads to despair and utter hopelessness. The other, to total extinction. Let us pray we have the wisdom to choose correctly.

> — Woody Allen,
> "My Speech to the Graduates" (1979)

At other times, a writer may adapt the highly formal prose rhythms of another century to the description of his or her personal experiences. Such adapting is possible because many of the great prose models from earlier centuries are still being read. Perhaps no text has had as much impact on the development of modern style as has the King James Bible of the seventeenth century. Consider:

> One generation passeth away, and another generation cometh: but the earth abideth for ever. The sun also ariseth, and the sun goeth down, and hasteth to his place where he arose. . . . All the rivers run into the sea; yet the sea is not full; unto the place from whence the rivers come, thither they return again.

> — Ecclesiastes 1.4–7

Such beautifully modulated sentences echo in twentieth-century styles whose subject matter is far more personal and

secular. The echoing occurs by means of formal parallelism
(i.e., a series of evenly balanced phrases) and as rhythmic
use of conjunctions — especially *and* and *but*. The effect can
be a slightly incantatory quality in the sound of the author's
language. Here is one example:

> There is never any ending to Paris and the memory of each
> person who has lived in it differs from that of any other. We
> always returned to it no matter who we were or how it was
> changed or with what difficulties, or ease, it could be
> reached. Paris was always worth it and you received return
> for whatever you brought to it. But this is how Paris was in
> the early days when we were very poor and very happy.

> — Ernest Hemingway, A *Moveable Feast* (1964)

Adapting the formal rhythms of the Bible to the treatment
of personal experience has led to some remarkable tonality
in recent literature. But it is also possible to go the other
way and apply the informal, broken rhythms of conversation
to subjects which might ordinarily call for highly formal or
"textbook" prose. Authors who want to make obscure topics
interesting to general readers may sometimes carry a conversational tone to extremes. Consider, for example, how the
contemporary journalist Tom Wolfe describes the deck of an
aircraft carrier:

> This was a *skillet!* — a frying pan! — a short-order grill! —
> not gray but black, smeared with skid marks from one end
> to the other and glistening with pools of hydraulic fluid
> and the occasional jet-fuel slick, all of it still hot, sticky,
> greasy, runny, virulent from God knows what traumas —
> still ablaze! — consumed in detonations, explosions, flames,
> combustion, roars, shrieks, whines, blasts, horrible shudders,
> fracturing impacts, as little men . . . skittered about on the
> surface as if for their very lives (you've said it now!), hooking
> fighter planes onto the catapult shuttles so that they can
> explode their afterburners and be slung off the deck in a
> red-mad fury with a *kaboom!* . . .

> — The *Right Stuff* (1979)

Tonal variety gives charm to language. The tones you prefer are often a matter of taste — or, more precisely, of auditory instinct. We all have our preferences among the stylistic possibilities. But no matter what sort of tone a writer conveys, the text ought to be heard.

Become Aware of Contrasts

It is said that there are two sides to everything. As a reader you should become aware of the contrasts within a text. The inner structure is bound to reveal a play of opposites that close reading uncovers.

Finding out the major contrasts is often necessary if you are to figure out what the whole text is about. To read Plato, for example, is to enter a world in which the contrast between body and spirit may show up everywhere. To study a textbook on physics is to enter a field where matter and energy, motion and stasis, expansion and contraction, interact. Even a letter congratulating you on your admission to a college implies a binary opposition: success/failure. The letter makes the "success" side dominant. But your awareness of the other side of the coin — the failure over which your success prevails — is in part what makes reading the letter a source of relief.

Recognizing key contrasts in texts is not necessarily hard. Sometimes the very titles disclose them. Famous examples include Matthew Arnold's *Culture and Anarchy*, Leo Tolstoy's *War and Peace*, Sigmund Freud's *The Ego and the Id*, Margaret Mead's *Male and Female*, and so on. But more often than not, the contrasts are revealed only within the texture of the writing itself. In such cases you must search for them.

Sometimes oppositions appear within single sentences. Those sentences possess the rhetorical quality called *antithesis*, which in some instances makes for memorable epigrams:

> The thoughts of the righteous are right: but the counsels of the wicked are deceit.
>
> — Proverbs 12.5

Ne'er look for birds of this year in the nests of the last.

—Cervantes

Hypocrisy is the homage that vice pays to virtue.

—La Rochefoucauld

Epigrams like those express bold oppositions. But contrast can acquire subtle complexity when the text is a work of sustained analysis. A contrast can reveal major unresolved issues that the text is concerned with. The author seems to turn to the reader and say: "This is what we must deal with or decide upon. How do you think we should proceed?" Consider the following excerpts:

The past is but the beginning of a beginning, and all that is and has been is but the twilight of the dawn. . . . A day will come when beings who are now latent in our thoughts and hidden in our loins shall stand upon this earth as one stands upon a footstool, and shall laugh and reach out their hands amid the stars.

—H. G. Wells, *The Discovery of the Future* (1901)

Chinese-Americans, when you try to understand what things in you are Chinese, how do you separate what is peculiar to childhood, to poverty, insanities, one family, your mother who marked your growing with stories, from what is Chinese? What is Chinese tradition and what is the movies?

—Maxine Hong Kingston, *The Woman Warrior* (1976)

[N]ow, in spite of all we have learned and achieved—or, rather, because of it—we hold this entire terrestrial creation hostage to nuclear destruction, threatening to hurl it back into the inanimate darkness from which it came. And this threat of self-destruction and planetary destruction is not something that we will pose one day in the future, if we fail to take certain precautions; it is here now, hanging over the heads of all of us at every moment.

—Jonathan Schell,
The Fate of the Earth (1982)

These passages, the last two of which appear deep within the texts from which they are taken, show the force of dynamic contrast at work. They are not "thesis" statements, but rather disclosures in passing of the major issues which the texts have come to face — and which the reader must face as well.

The contrasts within any text are an important part of that text's structure. To recognize them is an essential part of the reader's experience. Whether the contrasts are obvious or subtle, tenable or false, clearly resolved or left contradictory, the reader must decide. But to read a text without recognizing the powers contending within it is to ignore its world entirely.

Get to the Heart of the Matter

"Look to the essence of a thing," said the Roman philosopher Marcus Aurelius. However much time you spend, reading can seem pointless if it doesn't go all the way to the heart of the text. You may have skimmed the organizational features, inspected the various aims, and gotten to know the style and tone of the writing, but still feel frustrated if you haven't reached the essence of the thing. All progress in your relations with a text, from the first awareness of its existence to a close and sustained reading, should be aimed at discovering the text's heart.

The problem is that "heart" can mean different things, depending on your critical viewpoint and reasons for reading. For some readers, the heart of a text may be a passage or series of passages that seem to tie everything together and coordinate the flow of ideas throughout the entire work. One assumes that every coherent text has such a heart within it, a point of focus where dynamic contrasts meet

and from which all subordinate ideas flow outward to the
distant pages from beginning to end. In this sense, the
"heart" may be simply the most powerful part of the text,
and you know when you are near it by the way it seems to
throb and pound with unusual significance. What you iden-
tify as that special part of the text, however, may depend on
what you are looking for as you read.

For example, someone who is studying systems of authority might regard the heart of the U.S. Constitution as that
part which creates three branches of government. Someone
else, interested chiefly in human rights, might see the heart
of the Constitution as being the Bill of Rights. And still
other readers, concerned mainly with the history of democracy, might point to the Preamble:

> We the People of the United States, in Order to form a
> more perfect Union, establish Justice, insure domestic Tran-
> quility, provide for the common defence, promote the gen-
> eral Welfare, and secure the Blessings of Liberty to ourselves
> and our Posterity, do ordain and establish this Constitution
> for the United States of America.

Whether you see this passage or another as the "heart" of
the Constitution may depend on your viewpoint and interests. Eventually you will focus on passages that address
your reasons for reading the text. But the important thing is
to search for the lines that determine the heart of the matter — for you.

Passage hunting is an activity that most readers instinc-
tively pursue. In any sort of communication, after all, the
recipient wants to get the main message. Nonfictional texts
are usually more forthright than fictional ones in helping us
to recognize that message. They are often designed to expose
the governing thesis and its major arteries of argument and
demonstration. In works of fiction the key passages may be
as unpredictable to the author as they are to the reader,
having been written impulsively as part of the imaginative
development of the story. But whatever sort of text you are
reading, it is helpful to come away from it with some

reasonable idea of where the heart of the matter lies. Which passages you think are most significant may determine your critical viewpoint in future discussion. They may also determine how your understanding of the text differs from interpretations made by other readers.

Besides the search for key passages, there is another sense in which the term "getting to the heart of the matter" applies. The "heart" can be viewed as a sort of overall personality that characterizes the text. Finding the heart of the matter in this sense means coming to realize what the writing is *all* about. That sort of understanding is a reward for careful, diligent, and sensitive reading of the whole text; it can rarely, if ever, be achieved by a quick skim across the surface. In fact, not even slow and studious reading ensures that it will occur. There are some texts whose full identities remain hidden from us no matter how hard we try to know them.

But on the best occasions and as a result of our patient attentiveness, the heart of a text may reveal itself in the fullness of its meaning, both logical and emotional, and make us feel that we truly *know* what we've read. Then it is not simply a matter of particular passages but of everything at once. The process of criticism, which must deal in particulars, can never adequately describe this complete sense of awareness; it is something that each reader must feel alone. But it is precisely because you have been attentive to particulars and searched bravely for the heart of the matter that such moments will arrive for you.

Sense What May Be Missing

Let us say that you have just finished reading something long and difficult. How has the experience made you feel? Are you joyful or depressed, fascinated or indifferent, proud of your new knowledge or left in doubt? Are you bewildered, wishing to understand what the effort has meant to you? Are you conscious of a change in your life? Have you fallen in love with the text?

Of the many responses that reading can inspire, a few may be strong while plenty of others remain inactive. The intensity of your feelings is important, but so is the absence of those emotions which a text might have brought you but did not. If you enjoyed the reading but sense no regret that it is over, maybe you have more to gain from the company of others. Or perhaps you are glad that it's over; the text may have bored you and left you cold. At least you know what doesn't attract you at the moment. Some experiences are bound to be disappointing. As the American novelist Henry James once put it:

> [H]owever incumbent it may be on most of us to do our duty, there is, in spite of a thousand narrow dogmatisms, nothing in the world that any one is under the least obligation to *like* — not even (one braces one's self to risk the declaration) a particular kind of writing.

James's point here is that a single reader's impressions may not be those of the majority. However popular a text may be, your own heart is not a liar. The question is not what the text means to others, but what it means to you.

Knowing what a text means to you depends on your sense of what is present or missing in the relationship you've just concluded. But remember that you contributed to that relationship yourself. As a reader, you have gone from seeing the text as a distant object to making it part of your personal experience. During the reading you probably contributed your own thoughts, filled in "gaps" with previous knowledge that you brought to the occasion, and maybe even had a few arguments with the author. Your relationship with a text is always something that you and the text have built together. Therefore, you may have to share some responsibility for what is "missing" once the reading is over. But you should also give yourself plenty of credit if the reading has increased your knowledge or brought you pleasure. For again, the reader's experience is largely of the reader's own making. The text alone could not have been responsible.

Still, knowing what a text means to you is not always easy. It can be hard to say what you think about something you've read, just as it can be hard to describe other kinds of personal experience. Only in cases where you feel little or nothing does the problem allow for an easy solution. "Life being very short, and the quiet hours of it few," said the historian John Ruskin, "we ought to waste none of them in reading valueless books." If you feel nothing at all about a text, its value for you may be zero.

The main difficulties come with the valuable ones that you can't forget: the texts you enjoyed reading or that made a difference in your life. In such cases, not your feelings but the text itself can be what is missing. Reaching the end of a favorite book can be a bittersweet moment. Separation can be difficult when strong memories remain. At such times, the best thing to do is talk about it. That is what criticism does.

The rest of this book offers principles to apply as you interpret and evaluate your reading of a text. In general, those principles are simple guidelines for putting things in perspective. The text may be behind you, but its meaning and value may not be. The challenge now is to recognize that your first feelings about the text may not be the whole story. What you have read may seem wonderful or terrible or simply so-so, but you need to examine why. Then you will be a critical reader in the full sense of that term.

PART TWO

Interpreting

Chapter 3

The Need to Discuss

Of course, there won't be time to discuss everything you read. Usually you must limit yourself to texts that seem important and which, because of the special status you choose to give them, call for review and analysis. By talking or writing about those special texts, you can make them part of your education. Discussing them also begins the process of criticism, which in turn is a natural extension of the act of reading. There is a sense in which no relationship with a text is complete without a follow-up analysis of what the experience has meant.

What Is Critical Discussion?

Critical discussion first means responding to the text— analyzing what it says and evaluating its importance for you. The discussion may be oral or written. To have a meaningful oral discussion you must of course be with others who have read the same text. That opportunity occurs often in college classrooms, as well as in other circumstances, such as business meetings where a document is being studied. Less formally, you might find yourself talking over a letter or newspaper article with friends or family. But discussion need not require the presence of others. It might be a matter of writing down what you think, responding on paper to work out your thoughts. Forms of solitary discussion include notes, diaries, and critical essays (see Chapter 9). But whether your response is oral or written, the critical discussion will usually include two key elements: interpretation and judgment.

What Is Interpretation?

Interpretation is a way of discovering what the text means to you. Some people think it only means summarizing in a few words what the entire text is about. But there's more to it than that. Interpretation involves *re*reading to explore various aspects of the text and then selecting points for emphasis. This *re*reading is different from the first reading because it is influenced by your memory of what happened the first time. Then you were like a tourist gathering first impressions, but now you are a return visitor looking for those places that carry the most weight in your memory. When you have found them again and studied them more closely, you can begin to analyze their significance for you. Interpretation is thus a selective procedure because it requires focusing on particular aspects of the text.

How Is Interpretation Different from Judgment?

Judgment means deciding what value or importance the text holds, whether for you or for other readers. Before you can judge a text, you may need to consider it from a number of angles to discover what those values might be. When you interpret you are sorting and weighing evidence upon which an eventual judgment might be based. To judge a text without first interpreting it carefully is unfair because the judgment will not have been "earned." Just as courtroom proceedings call for close examination of evidence before a decision is handed down, critical reading calls for careful analysis before an evaluation is made. Judgment therefore follows and depends on interpretation.

Why Is Interpretation Difficult?

Interpreting can be difficult because any text will give you a good deal of evidence to sort through. Also, because your reading is a personal activity, dependent in part on your own emotions and previous knowledge, some private analysis of your feelings and ideas may be necessary. Because each reader is different, there may be many viewpoints from which to discuss a text. Once you begin talking things over, you will probably discover that interpretations vary widely from reader to reader. Making your own case for how you interpret the text can therefore get you into arguments with other readers. Keeping up your end of the discussion may require not only that you *find* evidence to support your view, but that you *use* that evidence to develop a coherent and persuasive interpretation. Using evidence that way means developing a reliable method for interpreting the text.

How Can You Get a Handle on the Text?

Although each reader's personal response may be different, a shared *method of interpretation* can provide common ground on which to base a meaningful discussion. A method of interpretation is a way of looking at a text from a viewpoint that reflects more than exclusively personal concerns. In other words, it is a way of opening up the discussion to include one or more critical *perspectives* that other readers can share. Once you have a clear perspective to work from, you can begin to express ideas about the text and organize your discussion.

What Are the Major Perspectives on Any Text?

Although in theory there could be as many critical perspectives as there are readers, you should be aware of five major avenues of approach to any text. These five avenues are not new. They have been in use for centuries. But we can still share them as ways of approaching whatever we read. You will find them used separately or in combination, over and over again, by critical readers of all kinds. They are perspectives that can be applied to texts at all audience levels, from all periods of history, and across all disciplines. In short, they are the basic means you can use to work through the problems of interpretation that any text will present. Though they may not solve all of those problems, they will at least give your discussion method and direction.

Those avenues of approach are known by many names. Here we shall simply call them (1) the social perspective; (2) the emotional perspective; (3) the rhetorical perspective; (4) the logical perspective; and (5) the ethical perspective. The next chapter will examine how each works.

Chapter 4

Five Ways of Interpreting a Text

Interpretation can be frustrating if you don't know where to begin. Suppose you're in a classroom or other meeting place where a text is being discussed. Maybe the target is an essay or a chapter or a formal report of some kind. Though you've read the material as closely as others have, you feel awkward talking about it. You remember most of what you have read, but when it comes to commenting on its meaning or importance, you don't know where to start. You hear other people saying things, and you know you're expected to say something too. All of a sudden, the professor or discussion leader turns to you and asks, "What's your view?"

Silence descends. Faces stare at you. After catching your breath, you stammer a few words as chill perspiration bedews your forehead. Then the discussion moves on to someone else while you sit frozen, trying to recall what you said. You hope it sounded reasonable, but you're not sure. Could it be that you didn't have a "view" at all?

Nonsense! You probably had plenty of views, but you weren't used to organizing or expressing them effectively. What you lacked was a means of approach that would allow you to bring your ideas together.

In this chapter we review five ways of approaching a text of any kind. These are ways that apply across the disciplines and that form the basis of even specialized critical discussions.

Even though we shall be reviewing them here in brief and somewhat simplified terms, you'll find that they can be adapted easily to more advanced circumstances, depending on your needs and interests.

NOTE: *Before proceeding with this chapter, take time to read the three sample texts reprinted in the Appendix. In order to demonstrate the five critical perspectives, we shall need to refer often to those texts as models for practice. Besides, those three texts — Lincoln's* Gettysburg Address, *Joan Didion's "On Going Home," and Lewis Thomas's "Making Science Work" — are good examples of the kinds of writing which college students and other critical readers nowadays find themselves interpreting.* Those three texts represent respectively the "classic" document of historic reputation, the contemporary personal memoir, and the expository or argumentative essay. The skills you develop in discussing those kinds of texts will help prepare you for future critical reading across the disciplines.

THE SOCIAL PERSPECTIVE

Using the social perspective means discussing the text in relation to society. Just about everything you read has some social relevance. Invitations, legal contracts, letters, and advertising are obvious examples. In the case of essays, nonfiction books, and other demanding texts, you can begin to take a social perspective by answering a few key questions:

What Social Concerns Does the Text Reveal?

One way to answer this question is simply to think about what general function or usefulness the text may have. Magazine articles, for example, may be reporting on new trends, showing people how to do things, or giving opinions on subjects of popular interest. On the other hand, some texts have less obvious social relevance. A mathematics textbook may not reveal social concerns directly; but if you consider how necessary applied math is to technology we use, the social significance of polynomials or differential equations should be evident. Thinking about how a text is used by others is one way to discover its relation to society.

Another way of answering the question is to think about any problems or conflicts that the text may address. Because all writing involves contrast, you can reexamine a given text's contrasts to see if any of them is social in nature. Ordinary reading material may present obvious social contrasts, as when a magazine ad tries to convince you of the difference between the wise people who own a given product and the fools who don't. But in longer texts, the social contrasts may have to do with anything from family tensions to class conflict, generation gaps, professional rivalries, political differences, or even war.

If you have read the three sample texts reprinted in the Appendix, try to summarize the social issues raised within each. You may discover that in Lincoln's Gettysburg Address the most obvious social conflict is the Civil War, for as Lincoln reminds his audience: "We are met on a great battle-field of that war." But other social concerns are detectable as well. One student summarized them this way:

```
The author is also concerned about the
continuing struggle for equality and the
preservation of our nation, which is "dedi-
cated to the proposition that all men are
created equal."
```

The question of whether a government "of the people" will survive or perish is certainly a social issue, and so is the issue of slavery — a matter not directly discussed in the speech itself but implied by the allusion to the Civil War.

As for the other two models in the Appendix, you may find that Joan Didion's essay reveals social concerns having to do with family identity and the meaning of "home," while Lewis Thomas's essay focuses on the social uncertainties brought about by twentieth-century science. Is the American family what it used to be? Is technology our

friend or our enemy? These are matters which Didion and
Thomas address respectively. The social perspective allows
you to focus on those issues as you discuss their essays.

Not everyone will agree on exactly how a text's social concerns should be summarized. But to make the effort is to
begin using the social perspective as an approach to the text.
When you've discovered what you believe are the key social
issues, you can move on to another question that the social perspective calls for:

How Does the Text Relate to the Past?

In considering whatever social concerns a text reveals, you
might ask how the text relates to the times during which it
was written. Newspaper articles are an obvious example of
how nonfiction depends on the world around it. In the case
of books, essays, and other less "news"-oriented texts, the
relation of text to history may be more subtle. Yet most
writing does reflect the author's awareness of his or her
times. Scientific writing, for example, may not always seem
concerned with the society around it, but the scientist's findings will be influenced by the current state of research in his
or her century. More personal writing, such as memoirs and
autobiographies, often comments on social trends that the
author has witnessed.

Consider again the three texts in the Appendix. Joan Didion's "On Going Home" is a product of the 1960s. The
author takes her times into account by speculating on
whether she is a member of "the last generation to carry the
burden of 'home,' to find in family life the source of all
tension and drama" (par. 2). Lewis Thomas, whose essay ap-
peared in the early 1980s, also takes history into account by
surveying the past 300 years of science in contrast to the
rapid developments of the past half century (par. 2). And, of
course, we can't overlook Abraham Lincoln's famous allusions to historical events as he saw them in 1863: the founding of the nation "four score and seven years ago"; the battle
at Gettysburg; and the unresolved fate of the nation during

the Civil War. If you ask yourself whether a given text has something to say about the times before or during which it was written, the answer will often be *yes* — maybe even *a great deal!*

There is still another question you can ask from a social perspective, and it is this:

How Does the Text Relate to Right Now?

Important as it is to consider how a text relates to the past, even more important may be how it relates to the present. If you've just read this morning's newspaper, the relation between the text and "right now" may seem obvious. In college, however, much of what you read may have been written months, years — even centuries ago. For that reason you should be ready to ask whether the social concerns raised by a text still affect us.

This question may cause you to emphasize matters that earlier audiences might have found less central to the text. For example, the crowd listening to Lincoln's 1863 speech probably felt that the key concern was whether the Civil War could be won by the Union forces. Today we know the answer to *that* question, and so we may choose to focus on broader concerns raised by the speech, such as freedom and the aims of government. Is the Gettysburg Address still relevant to American society in the late twentieth century? Here is what one student said:

```
I find this speech very moving.  The racial
issue was a powerful and destructive force
then--it still is.  As a nation, we've come
a long way.  As a world, we have so far to
go in matters of race, religion, and gen-
der.  For our nation, it seems the march
was openly begun with this war, with this
speech.
```

If you agree that Lincoln's words still challenge us to preserve democracy, you'll have a basis for discussing how this old text addresses the present.

What about works of more recent vintage, such as essays or books written within the past few decades? Here the question may be whether the social concerns raised by the text still reflect current behavior or practice in matters of custom, social activity, fashion, science, business, or whatever the subject may be. You may have to do some sifting to decide what still applies. In the case of Lewis Thomas's essay, you might be aware that scientific funding from business and government has increased since the essay was written, but still find timely the author's point about the continuing need for basic research. And in considering Joan Didion's "On Going Home," you might find the allusion to a girl dancing topless on crystal a bit dated; nevertheless, you could still find the author's uncertainty about the meaning of "home" relevant to the 1990s.

Summary

Discussing things from a social perspective allows us to view a text in relation to the world around it. By focusing on a text's social concerns as they apply to both the past and "right now," we may find that we already have plenty to say. But there are at least four other useful ways of approaching what we've read.

THE EMOTIONAL PERSPECTIVE

A second way of looking at a text is from a psychological viewpoint, or what we might simply call the emotional perspective. Though some texts seem emotionless (a legal contract, for example), most writing appeals to human feelings in one way or another. Focusing on a text from an emotional perspective can reveal new areas for interpretive discussion.

Does the Text Contain Objects of Emotion?

First, look for objects that the text invests with strong emotional significance. In the Bible, for example, such objects include the apple that tempts Adam, the Ark of the Covenant, and the Cross in the New Testament. While poetry and other kinds of imaginative literature are usually rich in emotive symbols, even nonfiction will sometimes display objects of emotion to signify moods or attitudes within the text.

In Joan Didion's "On Going Home," we come across several such objects: the contents of a drawer (par. 3), the telephone (par. 4), the vandalized cemetery (par. 4), and the sundress from Madeira (final par.). In context, those objects become associated with moods of nostalgia, uncertainty, dread, and hope — or, at least, those are general terms that might be used to describe their effects on the author. We can see that Didion is using those objects as symbols to intensify the emotional dynamics of her very personal essay. Consider also this from paragraph 3: "Paralyzed by the neurotic lassitude engendered by meeting one's past at every turn, around every corner, inside every cupboard, I go aimlessly from room to room." This eerie and rather discomforting sentence suggests that the ordinary objects in the house are for Didion more than mere objects of sentiment. They become associated with a "lassitude" that slows her down as she moves among them.

The more impersonal the writing, the fewer objects of emotion we might expect to find. However, if you look closely at Lewis Thomas's "Making Science Work," you'll notice how the author describes scientific discoveries as moments of "surprise" (final par.). Also, early in the essay he calls attention to the hostile emotions of those who distrust science itself:

> Voices have been raised in protest since the beginning, rising in pitch and violence in the nineteenth century during the early stages of the industrial revolution, summoning urgent crowds into the streets. . . .

Here the author deliberately uses emotion-charged terms—"protest," "violence," "urgent crowds"—to characterize science's detractors as being like an angry mob. Fair or not, this characterization dramatizes the contrast Thomas wants to draw between his opponents and scientists like himself.

Finally, consider the Gettysburg Address. Here Lincoln underscores the solemnity of the occasion by alluding to a single object—the battlefield. It has become "a final resting place for those who here gave their lives." For Lincoln the field is a symbol of sacrifice, but also, he tells us, a point of departure from which the living can take "increased devotion."

Naming and discussing the objects of emotion found in a text should help you to develop an interpretive analysis. But there is more to the emotional perspective than identifying a few key objects and the moods associated with them. Often there are several contrasting emotions to deal with, and for that reason we should pay attention to any emotional conflicts within the text.

Do You Find Evidence of Conflicting Emotions?

Since contrast is necessary to the structure of any text, we may well find that part of the contrast is emotional. In the Biblical story of Eden, for example, the apple may at first seem to signify temptation. But once Adam has sinned, the emotional picture grows very complicated. If we study the Eden story from an emotional perspective, we find many conflicts being raised: desire versus loyalty, pleasure versus pain, innocence versus guilt, and so forth. By recognizing those emotional contrasts we can learn something about the emotional *range* of the text.

When Abraham Lincoln tells his Gettysburg audience that "in a larger sense, we can not dedicate—we can not consecrate—we can not hallow—this ground," he is introducing an emotional conflict of sorts. The respect for the dead soldiers is so profound that the mourners are incapable of enacting that respect merely by dedicating the cemetery.

The soldiers have already consecrated the ground "above our poor power," as Lincoln puts it. He then *resolves* that emotional conflict by turning from the dedication of the cemetery to a greater alternative: the dedication of ourselves: "It is rather for us to be here dedicated to the great task remaining before us. . . ." In other words, we must turn from mourning to a spirit of new commitment. Lincoln's appeal to his audience thus moves from one emotional plane to another, challenging the audience to share in a transition from sadness to hope.

Sometimes the emotional conflicts within a text are left unresolved. In "Making Science Work," Thomas contrasts the "surprise" of pure scientific discovery with the desire of society for predictable technological advances. The author cannot tell us where this conflict of interests will lead, exactly, but he does assure us that the surprises won't stop coming: ". . . we will not be able to call the shots in advance" (final par.). Similarly, in "On Going Home," Joan Didion describes emotional tensions between her husband and her family, between her two senses of "home," and between one generation and another. But she does not tell us how those tensions will be resolved.

It's important to realize that many texts do leave emotional conflicts unresolved, sometimes because they must. A text isn't a failure or poorly written just because it doesn't offer a solution to every problem it poses. Emotional conflict within writing is known as *irony* (a literary term for the balancing of opposites), and many fine works are full of emotional ironies. We can't as readers be expected to resolve all of those ironies any more than we can expect the author to do it for us, but we can share the author's awareness of conflict and thereby move closer to a sympathetic understanding of the text.

What Is the Tone of the Author?

The word *tone* refers to the attitude of the author toward the subject he or she is writing about. Even when particular objects in the text become associated with particular emotions, and even when the text contains emotional conflicts, we may find that the overall work takes on a tone which we may infer as characteristic of the author. Thus, for example, we might say that Lincoln has a "solemn" tone throughout the Gettysburg Address, that Joan Didion writes "wistfully" about her family home, or that Lewis Thomas's writing conveys a tone that is serious but lively.

Characterizing tone is bound to be a subjective exercise on the part of the reader. That is because we infer tone from our personal responses to the subject matter of the text. Also, when we describe tone we allow ourselves to generalize about what are really many separate aspects of the writing: content, diction, prose style, and so forth. But even though describing the author's tone may be risky, no discussion of a text from an emotional perspective can be complete without our taking the chance. For of all the emotions that may be present in the text, it is the author's own that are likely to affect us most.

Summary

The emotional perspective considers whatever objects of emotion may be present, any emotional conflicts that may arise within the text, and finally the author's overall tone. It's important to remember that sometimes the emotions of a text vary, and that we cannot always expect emotional conflicts to be neatly resolved.

THE RHETORICAL PERSPECTIVE

Rhetorical analysis takes as its focus the form and style of the writing. Here, rather than concerning yourself with the social and emotional issues that might be raised, you give your attention to *how* a text is constructed. If you want to learn to write well, you can benefit from applying the rhetorical perspective. That is because rhetoric has to do with skills employed by writers to achieve desired effects. By looking carefully at the form and style of particular texts, you can discover ways to advance your own writing skills. In fact, you will find yourself appreciating more fully the *art* of writing.

Here are some questions you can ask to begin using the rhetorical perspective:

How Can the Text's Form Be Described?

Describing *form* means recognizing categories to which the text may belong. For example, you can begin by asking yourself whether the text is nonfiction or imaginative literature. If you know it's nonfiction, go on to categorize it by *genre*. Is it an essay, a speech, a biography, an editorial, a technical operations manual, or what? If it is a work of imagination, is it poetry, drama, or prose fiction? More specifically, is it a lyric poem, an epic, a short story, a novel, a tragedy, a comedy, or what? If you are in doubt as to the definitions of the various genres and subgenres, you can consult a handbook of literary terms for help. To know why a text belongs to a particular category, you need first to know how that category is defined.

The term *essay*, for example, denotes a short, nonfictional prose work that comments on some aspect of reality. As a form, the essay goes back at least as far as the sixteenth-century *essais* of Michel de Montaigne. That French author asked himself, "What do I know?" His many essays become answers to that question, commenting on subjects from war and politics to religion and literature. Today the essay is a popular means of exploring what *we* know about the various disciplines and experiences that affect our lives. In general, we come upon two kinds of essays: those that are *personal*, involving reminiscences about the author's own past; and those that are *impersonal*, containing little or no reference to the author's private life.

Joan Didion's "On Going Home" is an example of a personal essay, while Lewis Thomas's "Making Science Work" is an impersonal one—at least in terms of its subject matter. We find that Didion's essay refers often to her family, her home(s), her special memories, and her own identity in relation to what she has witnessed. By contrast, Lewis Thomas's essay tells us nothing about the author's private life; instead, the focus is on a public controversy having to do with science and technology. What Thomas writes does of course reflect his personal views and judgment, but his own personality is not the focal point of the essay.

Another subgenre of nonfiction is the speech, or what is more precisely called *oration*. Speeches, too, can be either personal or impersonal, though the historic ones tend to be the latter. Lincoln's Gettysburg Address is not about Lincoln himself, after all, but about the future of the nation. If you look up a definition of *oratory* in a handbook or encyclopedia, you'll find that a classical oration contains three parts: an *exordium*, which appeals to the traditions or customs of the audience; an *argument*, which sets forth the main message and offers reasons for agreeing with the speaker; and a *peroration*, or summing up, that heightens or inspires the message. The Gettysburg Address is an unusually short oration, but it does contain all three parts if you look closely. The first sentence invokes the nation's past; the rest, except for the last sentence, argues on behalf of renewed dedication to national principles; and the last sentence serves as the peroration. In other words, this very short speech does follow the form of classical oratory.

Once you've identified the overall form of a text—as being a personal essay, a classic oration, or whatever—you are ready to go on with a more detailed analysis of the text's rhetoric.

Which Rhetorical Modes Do You Find in the Text?

We use the term *rhetorical modes* to describe methods of organizing writing to serve particular functions. Those functions may include describing, narrating, defining, comparing, contrasting, classifying, illustrating, summarizing, as well as persuading. All texts make use of at least some rhetorical modes, and the text's overall form may determine the kinds being used.

The kinds of rhetorical modes found in an essay, for example, may depend on whether that essay is personal or impersonal. Because Joan Didion's "On Going Home" is a personal essay, we might expect to find modes that help make her personal experience vivid. Those modes include *description* and *narration*. Describing means providing sense impressions having to do with sight, sound, taste, touch, and/or scent. Narrating means telling about a sequence of events. We find that both of those modes are used throughout Didion's essay:

> . . . I drive across the river to a family graveyard. It has been vandalized since my last visit and the monuments are broken, overturned in the dry grass. Because I once saw a rattlesnake in the grass I stay in the car and listen to a country-and-Western station. Later I drive with my father to a ranch he has in the foothills.

Notice that the quoted passage contains both descriptive images (the broken monuments, the dry grass, etc.) and narrative (visiting the cemetery, listening to the radio, etc.). Personal writing often blends description and narration artfully so that the reader can experience an event and at the same time become aware of the setting. Precise narrative-descriptive detailing is almost a necessity in personal essays, though other rhetorical modes may be present as well.

On the other hand, impersonal essays tend to employ rhetorical modes suited to research reporting. Those include *definition*, *summary*, *classification*, *illustration*, *process analysis*, and *comparison/contrast* (see the Glossary for further explanations of those terms). In Lewis Thomas's "Making Science Work," for example, we find *summary* occurring in the essay's opening sentence: "For about three centuries we have been doing science, trying science out, using science for the construction of what we call modern civilization." Elsewhere, Thomas makes use of *classification* when he reviews scientific developments in fields from biology to social science (pars. 4–11), and again when he discusses the types of institutions that support basic research (pars. 12–16). This sort of formal distinguishing among types or categories is characteristic of impersonal essays, or what we call *expository* prose. The aim is to expose differences and distinctions that help explain a problem and/or point to its possible solution.

If you look carefully at Lincoln's Gettysburg Address, you may find the chief rhetorical modes to be contrast (i.e., between past and present), definition (i.e., the greater meaning of *dedicate*), and summary (i.e., of the events leading up to the dedication ceremony). You may find others, too.

By identifying which rhetorical modes appear in a text, you can reveal what functions the text is performing. That is true not only of essays but of all kinds of writing. In analyzing fiction, for example, you'll probably find plenty of narration and description, just as you will in personal essays, for the aim of fiction is to bring you close to the lives of imaginary characters. Business documents, textbooks, and other kinds of expository nonfiction may be given to other modes, especially classification, definition, process analysis, and summary.

How Can the Author's Style Be Described?

As E. B. White once pointed out, style is always something of a mystery: "Who can confidently say what ignites a certain combination of words, causing them to explode in the mind?" We can analyze the grammar of a text's sentences for clues, and we can talk about the "tone" of the author's voice. But style, like personality, is likely to remain more than the sum of its parts. Our efforts to describe an author's style probably won't succeed completely. But that doesn't mean we shouldn't try.

A graceful prose style often reflects a writer's keen awareness of grammar. Smooth parallel structures — known as parallelism or coordination — are often regarded as virtues of style, whereas misplaced modifiers, mixed metaphors, and verbosity are usually seen as flaws. (See the Glossary for more about those terms.) Analyzing the grammar of sentences can teach you a great deal about what works and what doesn't.

Some prose styles can be described as highly "formal." That is, they're marked by evenly balanced sentence structures resembling the fine cadences of classical music. The Gettysburg Address has that kind of polished formality. Consider this sentence: "The world will little note, nor long remember, what we say here, but it can never forget what they did here." Obviously, we *do* remember what Lincoln said here, partly because he said it so well. The sentence shows fine coordination as he balances the rise and fall of clauses on either side of the conjunction *but*. The verb phrases are parallel in form (i.e., "little note" — "long remember" — "never forget"). Furthermore, the repeating of the word "here," which otherwise might seem verbose, works like a resounding chord because of the rhythmic spacing.

Less formal styles are often called "conversational" because they come closer to the varied rhythms and loose structure of everyday speech. That doesn't mean, however, that an informal style isn't carefully done. Consider this passage from Lewis Thomas's "Making Science Work":

> We will solve our energy problems by the use of science, and in no other way. The sun is there, to be sure, ready for tapping, but we cannot sit back in the lounges of political lobbies and make guesses and wishes; it will take years, probably many years, of research. Meanwhile, there are other possibilities needing deeper exploration.

Here, as in conversation, the language moves forward unevenly. The lengths of the three sentences vary, and within those sentences some clauses are much shorter than others.

There is a sort of stop-and-go urgency that gives emphasis to certain terms. Notice how Thomas writes "it will take years, probably many years, of research." The double stress on *years* seems deliberate, but also a bit hesitant. We seem to be hearing someone thinking aloud, letting his style reflect the natural course of his reasoning.

Often you'll find that a prose style falls somewhere between the high formality of Lincoln and the more conversational quality of Thomas. If you consider Joan Didion's style, for example, you'll find her a bit closer to Lincoln when it comes to balanced phrases within sentences, but much closer to Thomas when it comes to varying the lengths of sentences themselves. Notice how her essay ends:

> I would like to give her more. I would like to promise her that she will grow up with a sense of her cousins and of rivers and of her great-grandmother's teacups, would like to pledge her a picnic on a river with fried chicken and her hair uncombed, would like to give her *home* for her birthday, but we live differently now and I can promise her nothing like that. I give her a xylophone and a sundress from Madeira, and promise to tell her a funny story.

If you're tempted to say that the personal subject matter and the pronoun "I" make this style less formal than Lewis Thomas's, look again. The long second sentence is far more oratorical than conversational, building rhythmically on a series of parallel phrases. But you'd be right in saying that, like Thomas, Didion sharply varies the sentence lengths and thereby brings her prose style closer to the normal pacing of everyday speech.

Let's say that you've now looked at the form, rhetorical modes, and style of the text. There is still another matter to consider when you are using the rhetorical perspective:

What About Ambiguity?

As philosophers from Francis Bacon to Jacques Derrida have reminded us, language is ambiguous. The same word or term can be understood to mean different things to different readers or listeners. The word "pride," for example, suggests healthy self-respect to some persons, but to others it connotes the sin of overestimating what we deserve. Thus saying that someone is a "proud person" could be taken as a compliment or a rebuke, depending on the intent of the speaker and on the understanding of the audience. Dictionaries can supply us with general definitions, called *denotations*. But each reader also inteprets terms according to personal *connotations* — meaning his or her own previous experiences with those terms. As the semanticist S. I. Hayakawa once pointed out, if we hear the phrase "Bessie the cow," we are all likely to think of different cows. The full implications of this problem are far reaching. If all language is potentially ambiguous, no two readers will read a text in quite the same way, and even the same reader may read a text differently on different occasions.

If you accept the notion that any word may be ambiguous, finding ambiguities in texts should be fairly simple. All you have to do is point to any line and say, "This can be read in different ways." You'd be right. But as a practical matter, we can't pause to challenge every word or term we read. What we need to look for are those words whose ambiguity raises serious questions about the meaning of the whole text.

In considering this problem we should first distinguish between ordinary — or "bad" — ambiguity that results from stylistic faults, and a literary — or "good" — kind that enhances the quality of the text. Ambiguity of the ordinary "bad" kind can be caused by mixed metaphors, misplaced modifiers, equivocation, imprecise translation from a foreign language, or by verbosity (refer to listings in the Glossary). Ambiguity of the literary or "good" kind is another matter. Here the reader's uncertainty as to the meaning isn't caused by poor writing but, on the contrary, by the ability of the author to heighten or intensify words in a way that creates new levels of possible meaning for them.

One way to find these "good" ambiguities is to look for

terms that the author stresses as being hard to define. Sometimes a text will begin to raise questions about its own key words. Consider, for example, this passage from Joan Didion's "On Going Home":

> I am home for my daughter's first birthday. By "home" I do not mean the house in Los Angeles where my husband and I and the baby live, but the place where my family is, in the Central Valley of California. It is a vital although troublesome distinction.

Here the author gives us two connotations for the word "home." She tells us that she will be using the second one — home as the place where her family is — in this essay. But she also says that the distinction between the two senses of "home" is troublesome. Later in the essay, we find that Didion is still uncertain as to what "home" means:

> Sometimes I think that those of us who are now in our thirties were born into the last generation to carry the burden of "home," to find in family life the source of all tension and drama. . . . The question of whether or not you could go home again was a very real part of the sentimental and largely literary baggage with which we left home in the fifties; I suspect that it is irrelevant to the children born of the fragmentation after World War II.

In this second passage, the author no longer uses "home" to stand for her childhood house in the Central Valley of California. Now she associates the word with abstract ideas such as "burden" and the "tension and drama" of family life. But Didion cannot be sure that this wider, more abstract meaning still holds true for a post–World War II generation. Thus the meaning of "home" remains a problem throughout the essay. The author may be saying that one's sense of "home" depends on one's age and viewpoint, but that the ultimate meaning may be undecidable. In any case, we need to recognize that special ambiguity of the word "home" in this essay, for the difficulty of knowing what "home" means is largely what the essay itself is about.

The two other texts reprinted in the Appendix also raise questions about some of their own key terms. Lewis Thomas's essay is largely concerned with what "science" has come to mean in the modern world. He admits that part of the meaning remains unclear:

> Illumination is the product sought, but it comes in small bits, only from time to time, not ever in broad, bright flashes of public comprehension, and there can be no promise that we will ever emerge from the great depths of the mystery of being.

Science may not be only a matter of proving things, Thomas suggests, but also of living with uncertainty. As one example of that uncertainty, he points to the word "cell":

> For a while things seemed simple and clear; the cell was a neat little machine, a mechanical device ready for taking to pieces and reassembling, like a tiny watch. But just in the last few years it has become almost imponderably complex, filled with strange parts whose functions are beyond today's imagining.

Here, Thomas shows us that a scientific term like "cell" can be as ambiguous as an everyday term like "home." But by facing up to that ambiguity, the essayist can address not only the question of what the word has meant—but also the question of what it is coming to mean. The reader is invited to wonder right along with the author.

Consider, finally, the Gettysburg Address. Here the word "dedicate" is surely a key term. In one sense, the dedication of the cemetery is a social ritual for which the audience has gathered. But Lincoln quickly challenges that ordinary sense of "dedicate." In a larger sense, he says, "we can not dedicate . . . this ground." The brave soldiers, he reminds us, have already done so. Setting aside the dedicating of the cemetery, therefore, Lincoln instead uses "dedicate" in other contexts: for example, being "dedicated to the proposition that all men are created equal," and being a "nation . . . so dedicated." If we look carefully at Lincoln's repeated use of "dedicate" within the speech, we realize that he is doing more than just reviewing familiar connotations of the word. He is creating new meaning:

> It is rather for us to be here dedicated to the great task remaining before us — that from these honored dead we take increased devotion to that cause for which they here gave the last full measure of devotion — that we here highly resolve that . . . this nation, under God, shall have a new birth of freedom — and that, government of the people, by the people, for the people, shall not perish from the earth.

Here Lincoln has given new meaning to the word "dedicate." That new meaning inspires a commitment to ideals that transcend the hour of mournful commemoration. Being dedicated in the newer sense is a matter of "increased devotion." But the full sense of what Lincoln means by "dedicate" may be indefinable — a sublime ambiguity. For it remains a word among others, and those other words — "unfinished work," "task remaining," "new birth of freedom" — all point to an uncertain future when the present act of dedication must be fulfilled.

Ambiguity is thus an important issue in rhetorical analysis. Sometimes the question of what a text means comes down to the question of what a particular word means. If that word is important within the text but treated by the author as having different connotations, chances are that deciding what that word means is a challenge that the text itself is facing.

Summary

The rhetorical perspective allows us to discuss a text's form, its rhetorical modes, its style, and its words. Once we have considered those matters, we should have a pretty fair idea of how the text is constructed.

THE LOGICAL PERSPECTIVE

The logical perspective takes into account the reasoning used by an author to reach a conclusion. Sometimes that reasoning can be very complicated, as in, say, a treatise on physics or a detailed legal brief. At other times, logic may seem to have been suspended altogether, as in a fairy tale where things happen by magic. But in the course of reading standard nonfictional material, you'll need to look carefully at the text's logic as a basis for deciding whether or not you agree with the views expressed. Here are some questions you might ask.

What Debatable Issue Is Raised by the Text?

A debatable issue is one that allows for controversy. It is a problem whose solution has not been agreed upon by everyone before the text was written. Sometimes a text will raise several such issues, though all of them will usually cluster around a central problem.

What is at issue in the Gettysburg Address? Lincoln puts it very succinctly: "Now we are engaged in a great civil war, testing whether that nation, or any nation so conceived, and so dedicated, can long endure." For the audience listening at Gettysburg in 1863, the question of whether the United States could survive as a nation was surely an unresolved issue. The war was not yet won, nor was its outcome in sight. Many believed that the Union forces would prevail, but half of America was still in rebellion. How could the Union hope to win? Lincoln raises precisely that question.

Or consider Joan Didion's "On Going Home." Hers is a personal essay, not a work of formal argumentation. But Didion does raise a controversial issue when she speculates on whether she is part of "the last generation to carry the burden of 'home,' to find in family life the source of all tension and drama." At issue here is whether American values changed after World War II in such a way that the "tension

and drama" of family life lost much of its former importance. Obviously, not everyone would agree that such a
change occurred. The issue is open for debate, as Didion
recognizes.

Consider also Lewis Thomas's essay. Here the author is
addressing a general readership concerned about the future
of science. The author raises a controversial issue early in
the essay:

> Three hundred years seems a long time for testing a new
> approach to human interliving, long enough to settle back
> for critical appraisal of the scientific method, maybe even
> long enough to vote on whether to go on with it or not.
> There is an argument. Voices have been raised in protest
> since the beginning. . . . Give it back, say some of the
> voices, it doesn't really work. . . .
>
>   The scientists disagree, of course, partly out of occupa-
> tional bias, but also from a different way of viewing the
> course and progress of science in the past fifty years.

The issue, then, is whether science does "really work."
Thomas reminds us that while some people fear and distrust
science, others — scientists themselves — have a different
view. As readers we infer that the essay will go on to explore
this controversy in more detail, and of course it does so.

What Conclusions Does the Text Reach?

After discovering what issues have been raised, you want to
know what conclusions the text reaches about those issues.
Logical thinking about a matter of controversy often results
in a stated position which the audience is invited to share.
To analyze the reasoning by which that conclusion is
reached, you might begin by identifying the conclusion itself.

If the main issue raised by the Gettysburg Address is
whether a "nation . . . so dedicated" can long endure, the
main conclusion is that survival depends on the dedication
of the living to the "unfinished work" of the past. Lincoln
encourages his audience to share the belief that further sac-

rifice to preserve "government of the people, by the people, for the people" is necessary.

And if the main issue in Didion's "On Going Home" is whether the meaning of "home" changed following World War II, the conclusion seems to be that the meaning did indeed change. At the end of the essay, the author wants to give her daughter "home" in the sense of family picnics by the river, but instead she gives her a sundress from Madeira and a promise to tell a funny story. The symbolism here may suggest that in the author's view commercialism and the promise of "fun" have become substitutes for the "tension and drama" of family life.

In the case of Thomas's essay, the issue—whether or not science works—is one upon which the author has strong opinions. The major conclusion is perhaps found in this passage:

> Science is useful, indispensable sometimes, but whenever it moves forward it does so by producing a surprise; you cannot specify the surprise you'd like. Technology should be watched closely, monitored, criticized, even voted in or out by the electorate, but science itself must be given its head if we want it to work.

Much of Thomas's essay argues that while we may distrust technology, or applied science, we should recognize that basic scientific inquiry "works" if given the freedom to produce its surprises. The key to workable science, in the author's view, is respect for the difference between science and technology.

Does the Text Contain Sufficient Evidence?

Once you've identified issues and conclusions, you need to analyze the reasoning by which conclusions are reached. In effect, you now become a bit like a jury weighing the evidence.

When you ask whether a text contains "sufficient evidence," you are really asking whether that text gives convincing reasons to show why its conclusion is valid. To answer that question, you need to take another look at the reasoning. In general, there are two possible kinds of reasons any text can offer you: those based on deduction and those based on induction. Most texts of any length offer you both kinds, though one kind may predominate. Again, let's consider the three texts in the Appendix as examples.

The Gettysburg Address, like many speeches, is primarily a work of *deductive reasoning*. Lincoln's argument for continuing the Civil War is based on general principles, and his conclusion follows from the application of those principles to the issue at hand. In effect, he reasons that only the living can complete the "unfinished work" of democracy, that "we" are the living, and that therefore only we can complete the task begun by our founding fathers. If you sketched out this line of reasoning in the form of a syllogism, it would look like this:

Major premise: Only the living can save democracy.

Minor premise: We are the living.

Conclusion: Only we can save democracy.

Of course, Lincoln doesn't use quite those terms. But if you infer his reasoning from the speech, you can see that his argument for dedicating ourselves to the task ahead rests on the major premise that responsibility falls on the living.

The two other model texts rely mainly on *inductive* evidence to support their conclusions. Reasoning by induction means drawing conclusions from the observation of facts or data. Such reasoning is at the heart of most scientific writing. But it also shows up in more personal writing when an author sets out to interpret his or her own experience.

Joan Didion's "On Going Home" is packed with inductive evidence to show that times have changed — and with them the meaning of "home." Her writing concentrates on precise factual details: the contents of a drawer, the vandalized cemetery, the image of a girl dancing in a San Francisco bar, the telephone calling Didion back to another city, the fried-chicken picnics she remembers versus the xylophone and sundress she buys for her daughter. Contrasts between past and present occur even in the conversation she holds with her great-aunts, who no longer know where she lives. All of the essay's details contribute to a sense of loss, a hypothesis about the "fragmentation" after World War II.

It may be easy to see the validity of that hypothesis as applied to the author's own circumstances, which are after all the subject matter of the essay. But it may be wrong to go further and say that the text contains sufficient evidence to justify a general conclusion about society as a whole. After all, Didion is reasoning from a range of facts bearing on her own family; she can only wonder whether she is a member of the last generation to carry the "burden" of home. The reader, in turn, must decide on the basis of his or her own experience whether the speculation about society rings true.

Lewis Thomas's essay is also in large part a work of inductive reasoning, though the scope of that reasoning is more impersonal. To support his hypothesis about the need for science, Thomas surveys history and specifies facts about the challenges ahead. He also comments on the various fields of science—biology, aerospace, earth science, astronomy, and so on—and suggests how each is facing new horizons. He summarizes the inductive evidence by saying this:

> The doing of science on a scale appropriate to the problems at hand was launched only in the twentieth century and has been moving into high gear only within the last fifty years. We have not lacked explanations at any time in our recorded history, but now we must live and think with the new habit of requiring reproducible observations and solid facts for the explanations.

If you find the inductive reasoning in this essay convincing, you'll probably agree that we must now live with the habit of requiring "reproducible observations"—in other words, with the habit of science.

Thomas also argues that science must remain independent of technology in order to succeed. That argument may be more deductive than inductive, for it rests on the assumption that all scientific progress occurs as "surprise" and that "basic, undifferentiated science" is what makes surprise possible. Your acceptance or rejection of that line of reasoning will probably determine whether you agree that science and technology are as different as this essay concludes.

However well reasoned the argument of a text may be, almost any conclusion remains open to question or future debate. That is because logic alone cannot account for everything. Deductive reasoning depends on premises that in turn depend on the author's personal beliefs. Inductive reasoning depends on the ability of a hypothesis to apply in all future cases. Because deductive premises are "givens" based on faith, and because inductive hypotheses can be overturned by future exceptions to the rule, argument remains a process in which opposing views are always possible.

Does the Text Take Opposing Arguments into Account?

In formal debate of the kind practiced by lawyers and college forensic teams, taking opposing views into account is always important. Often one side will summarize the opponents' reasoning, then attack it for containing errors or omissions. *Fallacies* are formal charges made against an opponent's reasoning; they include question begging, hasty generalization, stereotyping, and so on. (See the Glossary for a more complete list.) Making fallacy charges against someone else's argument is a bit like throwing punches in a boxing match, and usually there is plenty of punching from both sides.

However, most argumentative texts that you read are not structured like formal debates. There is no rule which says that an author must take into account every possible counterargument and refute it. Consequently, you may find that the attention paid to an opposing view is a minor or even nonexistent part of the text. Nevertheless, it's a good idea to search for any places where the author does allude to opposing views, for those places may give you clues as to which other lines of reasoning you might investigate on your own.

The Gettysburg Address is one example of an argument that does *not* take opposing views into account, at least not directly. Many readers have noticed how Lincoln avoids any mention of the Confederacy or of the South's argument for fighting the Civil War. One reason may be that the occasion did not call for it; another may be that Lincoln hoped to include opponents in his appeal for a "new birth of freedom." Because he does not attack Confederate logic in this speech, we can only wonder if Lincoln has his opponents in mind when he appeals to national idealism.

Texts that contain narrative writing will sometimes bring in opposing views by telling about persons who disagree — either with the author or with each other. In "On Going Home," Joan Didion presents her husband as an outsider who doesn't share her understanding of her family's home:

> Nor does he understand that when we talk about sale-leasebacks and right-of-way condemnations we are talking in code about the things we like best, the yellow fields and the cottonwoods and the rivers rising and falling and the mountain roads closing when the heavy snow comes in. We miss each other's points, have another drink and regard the fire. My brother refers to my husband, in his presence, as "Joan's husband." Marriage is the classic betrayal.

Like the reader, the author's husband hasn't shared all of her childhood experiences, and his more distant and sometimes uncomprehending view of her family home is perhaps closer to the reader's own perspective. He serves as a foil to the nostalgia that Didion feels, and his presence in the essay reminds us that there are other ways of looking at what "home" means. Late in the essay when he telephones to suggest that she "get out, drive to San Francisco or Berkeley," we are hearing a call to another way of life, a renewed involvement in the larger world beyond the family of one's childhood.

When it comes to exploring opposing views, impersonal expository essays are more likely to approximate the structure of formal debate. In Lewis Thomas's "Making Science Work," for example, the second and third paragraphs present two contrasting views of science: the first being the view that science "doesn't really work," and the second being the view of scientists who "disagree."

Though Thomas remains on the side of the scientists throughout the essay, he is careful to acknowledge the evidence cited by his opponents. At several points he draws attention to the problems and dangers that science has brought. He reminds us of the "radioactivity from the stored, stacked bombs or from leaking, flawed power plants, acid rain, pesticides, leached soil, depleted ozone, and increased carbon dioxide in the outer atmosphere." He also acknowledges that "[u]ncertainty, disillusion, and despair are prices to be paid for living in an age of science." By naming the drawbacks cited by his opponents, Thomas forces us to see the issue from two sides. He also helps his own cause by making his argument appear more objective than it otherwise might seem.

Besides introducing views opposed to his own on the question of whether science works, Thomas also summarizes disagreements between business and the academic community:

> Each side maintains adversarial and largely bogus images of the other, money-makers on one side and impractical academics on the other. Meanwhile, our competitors . . . have long since found effective ways to link industrial research to government and academic science, and they may be outclassing this country before long.

Here the author does not join one side or the other, but attacks them both. By saying that each side maintains "largely bogus images of the other," Thomas in effect charges both with the fallacy of stereotyping. He also causes the reader to wonder if reasoning on the basis of "bogus images" may prove costly to the nation's future.

Summary

Taking opposing views into account thus adds new dimensions to an author's argument. As a reader, you can study those opposing views for leads to other arguments that lie beyond the scope of the essay or book you may be reading. But remember that logical analysis is first a matter of studying the author's own argument: its issues, conclusions, and reasons offered as evidence.

THE ETHICAL PERSPECTIVE

You may feel that an interpretation should be over once the social, emotional, rhetorical, and logical factors have been taken into account. But there is one more important perspective to consider, especially if the text discusses or depicts human behavior. You should not overlook the question of moral values, or what might be called the ethics of the text.

Morality is a touchy subject to discuss. For that reason it is important to respect certain ground rules as you approach the whole matter. One is that you not attempt to impose your own moral values on the text. In other words, you shouldn't try to "read into" a text values that are not actually there. It is also important to remember that some authors do not advocate particular ethical positions but instead try to be objective or "unbiased" reporters. With those ground rules in mind, you should be ready to make use of the ethical perspective. Here are some questions to ask:

What Is the Highest Good Envisioned by the Text?

In moral philosophy the *summum bonum* — the highest good — is the ultimate ideal toward which ethical behavior is directed. Precisely what that ideal is can vary from person to person. However, the history of ethics suggests that duty, happiness, and perfection are among the most widespread concepts of the highest good. You might therefore begin by asking whether a text seems to aim at one of those three ideals, while keeping in mind that it may not.

Duty is an ancient and important ideal. When Moses carried the Ten Commandments down from the mountain, he may have brought with him the ethics of obedience. We find duty idealized by Socrates and the Greek stoics, by many religions, and by military codes throughout history. For the philosopher Immanuel Kant (1724–1804), duty is a matter of intuitive conduct. According to Kant's belief, you should "act only on that principle which you can at the same time will to be a universal law." This axiom, called the "categorical imperative," suggests that the individual should recognize intuitively what ought to be done — and then do it. Many philosophers have agreed that conscience is the basis for duty and that each person's struggle to obey the dictates of conscience leads to the highest good.

If we consider the Gettysburg Address, for example, it is easy to see that Lincoln is stressing the importance of duty. As one student put it,

```
Lincoln states that the people must "re-
solve" to continue to fight the war for
freedom.  Using the word resolve imparts a
sense of duty.  By his ending statement--
"and that, government . . . shall not
perish from the earth"--he implies that if
people do not continue this fight, the gov-
ernment which they created will not last.
```

Though Lincoln does not use the word "duty" as such, he admonishes his audience to be "dedicated to the unfinished work" and to preserve a government formed "of the people, by the people, for the people." Since duty may be defined as fulfilling one's sense of moral obligation to a cause, the Gettysburg Address is above all an appeal to conscience and a call to duty.

Happiness as the highest good is also an ancient ideal. The ethics of happiness (also called *eudaemonistic* ethics) dates back at least as far as Aristotle. Though there have been many disputes over what "happiness" may mean in particular circumstances, we may in general say that acts or ideas are aimed at happiness if their end result would bring pleasure or a sense of well-being. In our own time, many kinds of popular texts seem aimed at happiness. Travel magazines, self-help books, and light fiction may be obvious examples, though sometimes very serious literature also has happiness as a chief concern. In some cases, an author may reveal his or her longing for happiness by depicting its absence.

Throughout her essay "On Going Home," Joan Didion alludes to moments of past happiness and reveals her desire to pass on to her daughter the pleasures of family life. "I would like to promise her that she will grow up with a sense of her cousins and of rivers and of her great-grandmother's teacups. . . ." The regret that she can promise her daughter "nothing like that" suggests how deeply the author is aware of lost happiness. In an ideal world based on this essay's nostalgic vision, the highest good might be a perfect "home" that can be passed on from generation to generation. That such a home may now be out of reach does not prevent its remaining an ideal in this essay.

Perfection as the highest good is an ideal often associated with scientific progress. Philosophers such as Condorcet (1743–1794) and Auguste Comte (1798–1857) teach that whereas happiness may be an elusive goal, we can at least contribute to social and scientific progress and thereby help create a future perfection. Texts that report on ways to improve existing knowledge are thus often aimed at perfection as an ideal.

Thomas's "Making Science Work" might be viewed as such a text. The opening paragraphs of the essay suggest that science is flawed but "just at its beginning." Give science more time, Thomas urges. Give it time to perfect itself:

> What lies ahead, or what *can* lie ahead if the efforts in basic research are continued, is much more than the conquest of human disease or the amplification of agricultural technology or the cultivation of nutrients in the sea. As we learn more about the fundamental processes of living things in general we will learn more about ourselves, including perhaps the ways in which our brains, unmatched by any other neural structures on the planet, achieve the earth's awareness of itself. It may be too much to say that we will become wise through such endeavors, but we can at least come into possession of a level of information upon which a new kind of wisdom might be based.

Like many scientists before him, Thomas looks toward a future in which new discoveries, new capabilities, and ultimately new wisdom can be realized. The price for that future may be living with uncertainty, but we can dream of a time when our work will have paid off. Rather like Lincoln in the Gettysburg Address, Thomas asks us to consider our unfinished work. But whereas Lincoln reminds us of our national heritage in order to call us to duty, Thomas reminds us of our present ignorance in order to make us desire a perfected wisdom. "It is a gamble to bet on science for moving ahead," Thomas tells us, but in his view science is now "the only game in town."

Though duty, happiness, and perfection may not encompass all possible ideas of the highest good, they do often serve as signposts marking the main ethical routes along which many texts are moving. Even so, in looking closely at the ethics of a text we need also to consider specific convictions.

What Ethical Convictions Does the Text Reveal?

If we know which highest good the text seems aimed at, we can then ask what convictions are involved in the pursuit of that ideal. An ethical conviction is a belief about the rightness or wrongness of a particular way of behaving. There are many kinds of ethical convictions, but among the major categories are those which we may respectively call altruistic, egoistic, and political.

Altruistic convictions hold that the best way to do one's duty, achieve happiness, or reach perfection is by selfless commitment. That commitment may be to other people or to a cause deemed greater than oneself. Altruists in history include St. Paul, Joan of Arc, Mahatma Gandhi, and others who gave themselves wholly to the causes in which they believed. When Abraham Lincoln in the Gettysburg Address challenges us to be "here dedicated to the great task remaining," he is expressing an altruistic conviction. If we are to fulfill our duty to the nation, Lincoln tells his audience, we must give ourselves to the cause of preserving democracy.

Egoistic convictions have in common the belief that the highest good can be achieved through self-fulfillment of the individual. *Egoism*, or the concern with one's own destiny, should not be confused with *egotism*, or mere selfishness. An "egotistical" conviction may have to do simply with one's self-importance, but an egoistic conviction has to do with how one can best come to terms with oneself. "The good or ill of man lies within his own will," said the Greek philosopher Epictetus. And according to Henry David Thoreau, "What a man thinks of himself, that it is which determines, or rather indicates, his fate."

Because personal essays, letters, and other autobiographical texts tend to focus on the author's life, they can be expected to reveal some egoistic convictions. In Joan Didion's "On Going Home," for example, the author is concerned with her own identity in relation to her family and with how to face the changes in her life. Although she has an altruistic desire to give her daughter the same forms of happiness she herself experienced as a child, she comes to terms with the fact that present realities force her to behave differently. Perhaps it is just as well, Didion says, "that I can offer her little of that life." She will try instead to bring her daughter happiness in other ways, dependent on the newer circumstances of a postwar generation.

Political convictions relate the highest good to the welfare of the community. Such convictions range widely over the various ideologies that make up partisan politics and contrasting systems of government: Republicanism, Liberalism, Socialism, Monarchism, and so on. Obviously, the convictions of those political philosophies will vary with regard to specific issues. But you should at least recognize political convictions when you see them. They are different from egoistic convictions insofar as the latter stress the self working alone to fulfill ideals, whereas political convictions focus on group relations as the key to ethical behavior.

In "Making Science Work," Lewis Thomas states a political conviction when he calls for a closer partnership between industry and academic institutions:

> There needs to be much more of this kind of partnership. The nation's future may well depend on whether we can set up within the private sector a new system for collaborative research. Although there are some promising partnership ventures now in operation, they are few in number; within industry the tendency remains to concentrate on applied research and development, excluding any consideration of basic science. The academic community tends, for its part, to stay out of fields closely related to the development of new products.

Here we have a political statement that can't be neatly labeled "Democrat" or "Republican," liberal or conservative, but it is political nonetheless. Thomas is saying that if we are to perfect our science, we need closer relations between two sectors of the economy. Such closer relations might not have much to do with the politics of government, but they would have plenty to do with the politics of industry and with the academic politics of institutions. Moreover, if you were to disagree with Thomas on this matter, you would quickly find yourself involved in a controversy that could only be described as political.

Summary

The ethical perspective leads us to consider a text on the basis of ideals and convictions. Often a book or essay may present several ideals and many separate convictions. In some cases the author may boldly stress his or her own; in other cases ethical implications may be subtle. But even when the text does not seem to make an issue of ethics, the reader should search for whatever ideals may be implied — and whatever ethical convictions may be apparent.

REVIEW OF QUESTIONS TO ASK

The Social Perspective

What social concerns does the text reveal?

How does the text relate to the past?

How does the text relate to right now?

The Emotional Perspective

Does the text contain objects of emotion?

Are there emotional conflicts?

What is the tone of the text?

The Rhetorical Perspective

How can the form be described?

Which rhetorical modes do you find?

How can the author's style be described?

What about ambiguity?

The Logical Perspective

What debatable issue is raised?

What conclusions are reached?

Is there sufficient evidence?

Does the text take opposition into account?

The Ethical Perspective

What "highest good" does the text envision?

What ethical convictions are revealed?

Chapter 5

Consolidating Your Views

Let us say that you have taken time to reconsider a text from all five of the perspectives treated in Chapter 4. You have thought about the social concerns involved and how the text relates to past and present. You have identified objects of emotion, as well as any emotional conflicts, and you've characterized the author's tone. You've analyzed the text's rhetoric: its form, its modes of exposing information, its style and possible ambiguities. You've reviewed the issues, conclusions, and evidence that make up the text's logic. And you've considered the ethical ideals and convictions that the text may have expressed. You are now ready to consolidate your views into a coherent overall interpretation of the text.

There are essentially two ways to consolidate views. One is by engaging in open discussion with other readers, sharing ideas so that everyone contributes to a collective understanding of the text. The second way is more personal and independent. It involves working alone to decide upon which perspectives matter most to you under the circumstances, then writing about what you've read so as to emphasize the views you feel are most important. Let's consider each of those two methods in turn.

How Does Oral Discussion Help to Consolidate Views?

Getting together with others to talk over a text is one important way to consolidate views. Because different readers respond differently, a general discussion can reveal more ideas about a text than one person working alone is likely to come up with. Oral discussion can bring surprises, disagreements, and sometimes spirited arguments. But it can also help to build a consensus as to what matters most. If you've already considered a text from the five perspectives reviewed in Chapter 4, you should be well prepared to play a role in such a discussion.

Let's imagine, for example, a class meeting focused on Lincoln's Gettysburg Address. For brevity's sake, we'll assume that only a few students are involved and that no major disputes arise. To make things a bit more realistic, we'll also assume that some students are better prepared than others:

> *Professor:* So tell me, Mr. Vague, what do you think of the Gettysburg Address?
>
> *Mr. Vague:* Well, it's sort of important, I guess.
>
> *Professor:* Any other comments? How about you, Ms. Bright?
>
> *Ms. Bright:* Well, looking at the speech from a social viewpoint, you can see that it raises a concern about the future of democracy. That concern is still with us today. Lincoln is saying that we the living have to dedicate ourselves to the unfinished work of preserving a free society. I think that idea is important.
>
> *Professor:* Good point, Ms. Bright! Mr. Tardy, anything to add?
>
> *Mr. Tardy:* Yeah, well . . . not really.
>
> *Professor:* Mr. Eager, I see your hand is raised.
>
> *Mr. Eager:* I'd just like to add that from an emotional perspective, this speech is very powerful. I notice that it has a solemn tone, and I'm impressed by how Lincoln makes the battlefield an object of emotion. He moves his audience to feel humbled by the soldier's sacrifice, then inspired by the

thought that the survivors can dedicate themselves to a great cause.

Professor: Well stated, Mr. Eager. That brings us to the question of how the speech is constructed. Any comments on that, Ms. Carpenter?

Ms. Carpenter: According to my notes, the Gettysburg Address is one of the shortest speeches on record. But it contains all the elements of a classic oration. Lincoln makes masterful use of rhetoric as he contrasts the past with the present and depicts our nation's history as an unfinished process. The prose style includes beautiful parallelism — such as "of the people, by the people, for the people." It sort of gets to you like music.

Professor: What about ambiguity?

Ms. Carpenter: I'm not sure what Lincoln means by "conceived in liberty." Also, I'd guess that such terms as "dedicate," "created equal," and "new birth of freedom" might lead to a number of contrasting interpretations.

Professor: I agree. Let's turn to Lincoln's logic. Any thoughts, Mr. Swift?

Mr. Swift: Actually, I haven't read it yet. My car broke down and —

Professor: In that case, let's call on Ms. Reasoner.

Ms. Reasoner: I'd say the logic is mainly deductive throughout the Address. At issue is whether the Union can survive. Lincoln offers the premise that only the living can save the nation, then reminds us that "we" are the survivors who must do the job. The only fallacy I can see is that Lincoln thought the world would "little note, nor long remember" what he said. But that was a minor instance of question begging.

Professor: What about the logic of Lincoln's opponents? Does the speech deal with that?

Ms. Reasoner: Well, if I were a Confederate soldier at the time the speech was given, I'd probably feel that Lincoln's side wasn't the only one to represent the founding fathers' intentions. But Lincoln is not really addressing the South's arguments in this short speech. Also, of course, he doesn't deal with other possible objections, such as pacifist argument against war. But in a way he seems to be trying to include everyone in the ideal of preserving democracy.

Professor: Good point. Let's turn to the ethics of Lincoln's speech. Would anyone care to comment? How about you, Mr. Bored?

Mr. Bored: Lincoln believed in doing the right thing.

Professor: Your point is — ahem! — well taken. But would someone care to expand a bit? Mr. Wise, how about you?

Mr. Wise: I think Lincoln was calling on people to do their duty. He says that being dedicated to the future of democracy is what counts, more even than what's already been done. He expresses the conviction that we must look beyond ourselves and act for the good of the nation. That belief may sound old-fashioned, but it's worth thinking about.

Professor: Thank you, Mr. Wise. And thanks also to the the rest of you. I think we've reviewed some useful ideas here. Would anyone care to add anything?

Well, of course, *we* might add that this entire dialogue is a bit artificial. It isn't often that a discussion will move as quickly and rigidly from one perspective to another. Sometimes the questions raised may come from a discussion leader who deals with critical perspectives less directly or who emphasizes one perspective over others. Then, too, real participants aren't likely to sound quite like Ms. Bright, Mr. Eager, Ms. Carpenter, Ms. Reasoner, and Mr. Wise do here. But the point is that opportunities do arise to make use of the five perspectives and to consolidate those views through free participation. Preparing to summarize points from all five perspectives can help you to shine in discussion, while avoiding the embarrassments suffered above by Messrs. Vague, Tardy, Swift, and Bored.

Sharing ideas is, after all, the purpose of group discussion. The aim is to help each other realize things that might have gone unnoticed and thereby expand everyone's awareness of the full text. Although a group discussion may be conducted in formal circumstances, its outcome will always be a bit unpredictable. After all, the progress of a good discussion depends on our responses not only to the text but to each other as well.

How Can Working Alone Help to Consolidate Your Views?

Useful though oral discussion is, it does have some disadvantages. There may not be time enough to discuss everything in detail. Because talk is spontaneous, people may express themselves less clearly than they would if given a chance to reflect. It's hard to "edit" a conversation. Then, too, because some participants are more shy than others, there's a chance that not everyone will be heard from. For all those reasons, we cannot rely solely on oral conversation to consolidate interpretive views.

Working alone has several advantages. You are able to develop your ideas more completely, weigh points, decide which perspectives are most important to you, and then incorporate your thoughts into a coherent written commentary on the text. The act of writing about reading is discussed in more detail in Chapters 9 and 10. Right now, let's focus on two possible outcomes of that writing process: (1) specializing in one perspective and (2) blending a number of perspectives.

What Is a Specialized Viewpoint?

Specializing in one point of view means developing an analysis based on one major perspective. Oral discussion rarely allows for sustained treatment of a text from one point of view, but working on your own gives you the opportunity to develop a chosen perspective in detail.

For example, consider the following passage written by a student—a real one this time—to develop a social perspective on the Gettysburg Address:

```
Sometimes, in my opinion, an emotional plea
can be more influential than straight fact.
Lincoln draws attention and sympathy to the
```

```
men who died in war.  He uses phrases such
as ". . . that from these honored dead we
take increased devotion to that cause for
which they here gave the last full measure
of devotion."  By using words, like honored
and devotion, Lincoln stresses the honora-
ble aspects of the fight and gives the en-
couragement that the people need to con-
tinue their fight.  In a period when many
died, this speech helped to make the war
seem righteous to those still fighting.
```

Whether or not you agree with all of the thoughts presented in this passage, you can see that the writer is developing her analysis from an emotional perspective, including more examples than an oral discussion would normally allow. This working out of fine points is an important advantage that comes from specializing in one chosen perspective on a text.

In fact, scholars at a professional level often pursue specialized points of view as part of their research. Here, for example, is a passage from an article by Roy Basler, a distinguished Lincoln scholar who wrote about the Gettysburg Address from a rhetorical perspective:

> Computation shows that of the two hundred and seventy-two words in the address nearly half (one hundred and thirty-two, to be exact) are repetitions. For example, the pronoun *we* occurs ten times; *here*, eight times. Recurring in a variety of positions and with changing emphasis, they furnish Lincoln's theme of the preservation of democracy with a pointed meaning — *we*, *here*.

—from "Abraham Lincoln's Rhetoric,"
American Literature 11 (1939): 167–82

Basler carries the analysis of Lincoln's rhetoric much further than ordinary oral discussion ever would. But notice that this critic's painstaking study reveals an interesting point about Lincoln's repeated use of *we* and *here*. It's a point that would almost certainly be overlooked in ordinary conversation about the text.

Choosing to specialize in one or another perspective is an option that each reader has. Often, term papers, research articles, and even whole books of critical analysis evolve from concentrated attention to one or a few problems that a given perspective reveals. You can go a long way in pursuing just one point of view. However, it is also possible to consider a number of perspectives as you develop your discussion.

What Are Blended Perspectives?

If the first way to treat consolidated perspectives is to select one of them for special attention, the second way is to select several for a combined — or "blended" — application. Blended perspectives should not be confused with "blurred" perspectives, for to blend things well you need to keep your issues clear.

Consider the following excerpt in which a student blends emotional, logical, and ethical perspectives in commenting on the Gettysburg Address:

Whether or not a nation dedicated to liberty and universal equality can survive is the debatable issue Lincoln presents. His concluson is that it can survive if present and succeeding generations affirm the "full measure of devotion" advanced by those who struggled and died. By implication he reasons that to do otherwise would violate the founding concept of a national government based on popular commitment and choice.

The Gettysburg Address mirrors the belief my father instilled in me: here, a

```
person can find life's fullness if he's
willing to engage in unrelenting struggle.
Moreover, the Address alludes to a grim re-
ality: some seeds die so that the harvest
may eventually be taken.
```

Notice that this student's commentary ranges over matters that involve separate perspectives. The point about "the debatable issue" is concerned with the speech's logical dimensions, while the student's remarks about his father bring in factors that pertain to emotion and ethics. This kind of blending can be effective if the separate perspectives are still brought into focus, however briefly. Here the student has managed to achieve this focus by using specific examples to support his analysis: a direct quotation in the first paragraph and a proverb in the second.

Blending perspectives can widen the range of interpretation, but it can also lead to vagueness unless precise examples are given to support general statements. Also, an analysis can drift out of control if the writer doesn't stick to a main theme. That is why an experienced critic who blends perspectives will often allow one perspective to dominate, no matter now many others he or she brings in.

Consider the following passage written by Carl Sandburg, a Lincoln biographer, again about the Gettysburg Address. You'll notice that the passage blends a number of perspectives — social, emotional, rhetorical, and ethical — but that only one of those tends to dominate the entire commentary:

> . . . the Gettysburg Speech is one of the great American poems, having its use and acceptation far beyond American shores. It curiously incarnates the claims, assurances, and pretenses of republican institutions, of democratic procedure, of the rule of the people, and directly implies that popular government can come into being and can then "perish from the earth." . . . Apart from its immediate historic setting it is a timeless psalm in the name of those who *fight* and *do* in behalf of great human causes rather than

talk, in a belief that men can "highly resolve" themselves and can mutually "dedicate" their lives to a cause, in a posture of oath-taking that "these dead shall not have died in vain."

> —from "Abraham Lincoln" in
> *Literary History of the United States,*
> ed. R. E. Spiller et al.
> 4th rev. ed. (1974)

By comparing Lincoln's speech to a poem, Sandburg sets the stage for a number of remarks about the inspirational qualities of the Gettysburg Address. Those remarks touch on many aspects of the speech's rhetorical and ethical content. However, the overriding concern for Sandburg in this passage is surely the social perspective. He points out how the speech has its "use" far beyond American shores, that it embodies the principles of republican institutions, democratic procedure, and the rule of the people. He also stresses the function of the speech in honoring a special kind of social role: "those who *fight* and *do* in behalf of great human causes." But although Sandburg has allowed social aspects to dominate his blend of perspectives on Lincoln's speech, we shouldn't overlook the fact that several other perspectives are involved.

Let's take one more example. Below are excerpts from an article by the famous American literary critic Edmund Wilson. Here the comments do not focus exclusively on the Gettysburg Address, but deal more generally with Lincoln's qualities as an author. Again, however, we can see blended perspectives at work:

> His devotion to the United States was based on his firm conviction, derived from his own experience, that our system allowed a poor man to succeed. . . . If [Lincoln's] intellect was rigorous and his will tenacious, his emotional mood was despondent. He identified himself with . . . the suffering involved in the war, which, as President, he had to prolong.

. . . .

This brings us to Lincoln's style, which was highly developed in the literary sense and yet also instinctive and natural and inseparable from his personality in all of its manifestations. . . . [H]e is working for the balance of eighteenth-century rhythms, and he soon learns how to disembarrass these of eighteenth-century pomposity. He will discard the old-fashioned ornaments of forensic and congressional eloquence, but he will always have at command the art of incantation with words, and will know how to practice it magnificently — as in the farewell to Springfield, the Gettysburg speech, and the Second Inaugural — when the occasion and his own emotion prompt it.

— from "Abraham Lincoln,"
The New Yorker
14 Mar. 1953: 106–20

Edmund Wilson comments on Lincoln's convictions, mood, and style. He thereby blends ethical, emotional, and rhetorical perspectives. But if we were to say which of those perspectives dominates Wilson's commentary, we'd be justified in seeing the emotional perspective as paramount, at least in the excerpts quoted above. Wilson is closely observant of Lincoln's prose style and other rhetorical strengths, but he views the style as dependent on the psychology of the author. Lincoln will "always have at command the art of incantation with words," says Wilson, " . . . when the occasion and *his own emotion* prompt it." Here again, then, we have a blending of perspectives in which one concern weighs a bit more heavily than the rest.

Blending perspectives is an art learned through practice and experience. To become more familiar with how it's done, you ought really to study the work of professional critics. Every college library carries *The New York Review of Books, The Saturday Review*, as well as any number of scholarly journals and "little magazines" that feature review articles by skilled commentators. By reading such articles firsthand, you can learn a great deal about how critical perspectives work in practice. In general, you'll find that some critics take highly specialized viewpoints while others blend perspectives according to their interests. But you'll also find that there is a freedom about criticism that each critic enjoys. It is your freedom, too, whenever you're faced with the job of commenting on a text.

Summary

Consolidating your views can be done either through oral discussion or by working alone. Talking over a text with others can lead to new insights and help establish a consensus about what matters most to a group of readers. Working alone can help you to pursue an analysis from several perspectives, to explore fine points, and ultimately to produce a thorough critical response. That response may represent a specialized viewpoint that you've arrived at, or it may represent a blending process in which several perspectives are brought together.

Chapter 6

Using Perspectives Across the Disciplines

In theory the five perspectives reviewed in Chapter 4 can be applied to *any* text. Whether you're interpreting a speech, an essay, a textbook, or a novel—or for that matter an ad in the paper or a letter from a friend—you can always apply the social, emotional, rhetorical, logical, and ethical points of view. But in practice, as Chapter 5 has shown, you're not often likely to apply those five perspectives in a perfectly even, balanced way. Instead, you will find yourself selecting one or another perspective for special emphasis, depending on your own feelings about the text.

Which perspectives you choose to stress may depend on other factors, too. One of those factors is simply the kind of text you're dealing with. Some texts seem naturally to invite one perspective over another. A book on calculus, for example, demands to be interpreted from a logical perspective, for mathematical reasoning is what that book is mostly about. On the other hand, a newspaper article on African famine will inevitably call for social and emotional perspectives. The content of a text may have a great deal to do with determining the viewpoint(s) you choose to apply.

Another important factor may be the circumstances under which you're doing the reading. Let's say you've just read Charles Darwin's famous book *Origin of Species* (1859) as part of a course in biology. Chances are the focus of the course will cause you to study Darwin's book from a logical perspective, weighing the evidence the author presents for his theory of evolution. But suppose you've read the same book as part of a course in English history. Now you might find yourself becoming more concerned with the social and ethical implications of Darwin's writing. The point is simply that your choice of perspectives may well be influenced by the situation you're in at the time of reading.

Careers and formal education have a great deal to do with that situation. As a college undergraduate, for example, you'll probably be taking courses across several disciplines. Each course may carry its own kind of perspectival emphasis. Let us briefly consider how some major areas of study might relate to the perspectives we've reviewed in this book.

Which Perspectives Apply in the Study of History?

Here, as in all other disciplines, the first answer must be that *all* perspectives apply. Surely any historian's work — from the ancient writings of Thucydides to the latest history book on the market — can be looked at from social, emotional, rhetorical, logical, and ethical points of view. Yet it's also true that history in general is the "story" of human behavior across time. We might therefore expect that reading history will cause us to make special use of the *social* perspective.

Take, for example, the following passage in which the historian Barbara Tuchman is describing an event of World War I:

> On August 19 as the fusillade of shots cracked through Aerschot twenty-five miles away, Brussels was ominously quiet. The government had left the day before. Flags still decked the streets refracting the sun through their red and yellow fabric. The capital in its last hours seemed to have an extra bloom, yet to be growing quieter, almost wistful. Just before the end the first French were seen, a squadron of weary cavalry riding slowly down the Avenue de la Toison

evidence in terms of a formula. No "opposition" is taken into account here, though in other circumstances mathematicians do debate issues concerning the application of formulas.

Of course, to be able to apply the logical perspective to math or other fields where special symbols are used, the reader must first understand the meanings and uses of those symbols. That is why we might regard the *rhetorical perspective* as a prerequisite to the logical perspective when we're reading math and science. Because mathematics has its own "language," we need to adjust ourselves to the forms, modes, and styles of that language as a basis for comprehending its logical qualities. No student of science can expect to learn much without first paying attention to the fundamentals of scientific rhetoric.

Nevertheless, the logical perspective remains essential to mathematics and to physical sciences such as chemistry, physics, and astronomy. In all those fields, it is the logical working out of problems that captures the reader's interest. You may discover, however, that physical sciences differ somewhat from math by requiring more attention to the third and fourth questions that the logical perspective raises: that is, is the evidence sufficient, and are there opposing views?

Because the physical sciences study the behavior of objects in nature, the evidence gathered by such fields as chemistry and physics is mainly inductive data. Since such data can often be variously interpreted, different hypotheses arise as to the meaning and future value of the evidence produced. Texts devoted to the physical sciences often report on inductive experiments and discuss contrasting views of scientific problems. Take this passage, for example:

> Our modern picture of the universe dates back to only 1924, when the American astronomer Edwin Hubble demonstrated that ours was not the only galaxy. There were in fact many others, with vast tracts of empty space between them. In order to prove this, he needed to determine the distances to

these other galaxies, which are so far away that, unlike nearby stars, they really do appear fixed. Hubble was forced, therefore, to use indirect methods to measure the distances. Now, the apparent brightness of a star depends on two factors: how much light it radiates (its luminosity), and how far it is from us. For nearby stars, we can measure their apparent brightness and their distance, and so we can work out their luminosity. Conversely, if we knew the luminosity of stars in other galaxies, we could work out their distance by measuring their apparent brightness. Hubble noted that certain types of stars always have the same luminosity when they are near enough for us to measure; therefore, he argued, if we found such stars in another galaxy, we could assume that they had the same luminosity — and so calculate the distance to that galaxy. If we could do this for a number of stars in the same galaxy, and our calculations always gave the same distance, we could be fairly confident of our estimate.

—Stephen W. Hawking,
A Brief History of Time (1988)

As you can see, the author is summarizing the results of an astronomer's experiments having to do with space measurement. The passage reveals the importance of those experiments, suggests how they changed previously held beliefs, and describes the logical process by which the experiments were conducted.

Applying a logical perspective to scientific texts comes naturally to most students, for logic is at the heart of nearly all scientific discourse. But we shouldn't forget that other perspectives apply, too. Scientific experiments can raise ethical issues, for example. And, as in the case of math, the rhetorical perspective relates to the special terms and symbols that separate disciplines employ.

Which Perspectives Apply in the Social Sciences?

The social sciences — which include anthropology, economics, political science, and sociology — continue to invite all five of the perspectives we reviewed in Chapter 4. But because in a sense these fields stand midway between history and physical sciences, they often place a combined emphasis on the social and logical perspectives. Like history, fields such as economics and anthropology study human behavior over the centuries. But like physical science, they often stress the importance of gathering and interpreting experimental data. Thus when you read works in the social sciences, you'll find yourself applying social and logical perspectives routinely.

Here, for example, is a passage from a recent book in the field of economics:

> Friedman's theory of the demand for money uses a similar approach to that of Keynes and the earlier Cambridge economists, but does not go into detail about the motives for holding money. Instead, Friedman made use of the theory of asset demand to indicate that the demand for money will be a function of permanent income and the expected returns on alternative assets relative to the expected return on money. There are two major differences between Friedman's theory and Keynes'. Friedman believed that changes in interest rates have little effect on the incentives for holding other assets relative to money. Thus, in contrast to Keynes, he viewed the demand for money as insensitive to interest rates. In addition, he differed from Keynes in stressing that the money demand function does not undergo substantial shifts and so is stable. These two differences also indicate that velocity is predictable, yielding a quantity theory conclusion that money is the primary determinant of aggregate spending.
>
> — Frederic S. Mishkin, *The Economics of Money, Banking, and Financial Markets*, 2nd ed. (1989)

You'll notice that in this passage the author is contrasting the theories of two economists, Friedman and Keynes. Both economists address a social concern, in this case the demand for money, but their theories differ with respect to inferences drawn from observation. Thus the reader is being led to consider a logical argument over how an aspect of social behavior should be interpreted.

But again, you can't afford to ignore other perspectives that may contribute to your understanding. As with the physical sciences, you'll find that social sciences have evolved forms and terminologies that can seem foggy to the reader who hasn't taken the rhetorical perspective into account by way of preparation. Also, as might be said of all disciplines, the conclusions and arguments you encounter are subject to ethical analysis as well. You need to ask, finally, what "good" the text is aimed at and what moral implications are involved.

Which Perspectives Apply in the Study of Arts and Literature?

If we turn to the arts, often we'll find that the objects of study are imaginative constructs — paintings, sculpture, architecture, musical compositions, and other single works. Texts about those works are invariably analytical. Writers who study the arts are themselves critics, so that the texts you read will be applying interpretive perspectives much as you are doing, though sometimes in more sophisticated ways. Paintings, symphonies, and even cathedrals can be commented on from social, emotional, logical, and even ethical perspectives if historical and human factors are taken into account. But if we must generalize about which perspective is most common in the study of arts, we may be inclined to say that the *rhetorical* perspective tends to take precedence.

It's important to remember that the rhetorical perspective has to do with form and style. While the term *rhetoric* is mainly a literary term, we can say that things other than written texts are rhetorical, too, insofar as they possess forms and styles that can be analyzed. The word "rhetoric" may not often be used by art historians or music critics, but nevertheless you'll find that many commentaries on art do focus directly on form and style. Here, for example, is an art historian discussing a painting by Leonardo Da Vinci:

> While working on *The Battle of Anghiari*, Leonardo painted his most famous portrait, the *Mona Lisa*. . . . The delicate *sfumato* of the *Madonna of the Rocks* is here so perfected that it seemed miraculous to the artist's contemporaries. The forms are built from layers of glazes so gossamer-thin that the entire panel seems to glow with a gentle light from within. But the fame of the *Mona Lisa* comes not from this pictorial subtlety alone; even more intriguing is the psychological fascination of the sitter's personality. Why, among all the smiling faces ever painted, has this particular one been singled out as "mysterious"? Perhaps the reason is that, as a portrait, the picture does not fit our expectations. The features are too individual for Leonardo to have simply depicted an ideal type, yet the element of idealization is so strong that it blurs the sitter's character. Once again the artist has brought two opposites into harmonious balance. The smile, also, may be read in two ways: as the echo of a momentary mood, and as a timeless, symbolic expression. . . . Clearly, the *Mona Lisa* embodies a quality of maternal tenderness which was to Leonardo the essence of womanhood. Even the landscape in the background, composed mainly of rocks and water, suggests elemental generative forces.

> —H. W. Janson, *History of Art*, 3rd ed. (1986)

In this passage the author draws our attention to several aspects of the painting's form: its layers of glazes, its stylistic contrasts, and its symbolic shapes. The critic's aim is to describe the features which characterize the overall construction of the artwork, and at the same time to make us aware of the governing tendencies of the painter's style. This focus on constructive features is known as "formalism," a practice which corresponds to rhetorical analysis in literary criticism.

The formalist approach is also used by musicologists interested in analyzing harmony, rhythm, and other compositional features of music.

We should add that not all texts on art and music are purely "formalist." In the nineteenth century, for example, it was common for writers to study art mainly from ethical and social perspectives, relating the qualities of a painting or musical composition to the religious, traditional, or political values of the society from which the artwork came. In this century, too, we sometimes find critics commenting positively or negatively on the social, emotional, and/or ethical implications of art. That happens, for example, when certain artists or musicians are attacked for "obscenity" or "decadence." But it's probably true that in academic circles, at least, the study of art concentrates on form, and therefore invites mainly what we have been calling the rhetorical perspective.

Much the same is true in the study of literature, or what is more precisely called literary history. Here, the object of study is usually a text—a poem, a play, a novel, and so on—which, like all texts, is susceptible to analysis from all of the perspectives we've considered. But while you will find literary critics who specialize in social criticism, psychological criticism, logical analysis, and ethics, by far the most widely practiced critical approach in the past half-century has been rhetorical analysis.

You'll recall that the rhetorical perspective invites questions about the text's form, rhetorical modes, style, and possible ambiguities. Of these topics, it is the last matter—ambiguity—which seems to have fascinated twentieth-century critics most. What does a particular passage or term mean?—or what could it mean? That is the sort of question that language professors so often ask. You'll find that many articles and books that deal with the study of literature tend to concentrate on the analysis of difficult passages from famous texts.

Consider, for example, the following excerpt from a scholarly essay about the poetry of John Keats (1795–1821).

The critic quotes a passage from the poem she is studying, then follows with an analysis of that passage:

> *No, never more*
> *Shall airy voices cheat me to the shore*
> *Of tangled wonder, breathless and aghast.*

This farewell to "airy" imagination displays the choice that Keats at first felt compelled to make in deciding on a tragic and human art. He could not yet see a relation between the airy voices of visionary shores and human truth; and he felt obliged to choose truth. "I deem," says the narrator of Endymion, "Truth the best music." "Endymion," uneasily balancing the visionary, the symbolic, and the truthful, had nonetheless brought Keats to his view of art as necessarily related, though in symbolic terms, to human reality; as necessarily hieroglyphic; as the locus of social cooperation by which the symbol regained mimetic force; and as a social resurrective power.

—Helen Vendler,
The Music of What Happens (1988)

You can see here that the critic is commenting from rhetorical and social perspectives on Keats's poetry. More specifically, she is working to reveal the meaning of the term "airy voices." She is concerned not only with how that term applies in the poem quoted, but also with how it represents part of a philosophical contrast found throughout Keats's early poetry. This sort of close analysis of passages is called *explication*. It is a standard activity among professional critics.

Although the rhetorical perspective may currently dominate literary studies, such studies are never very far removed from the other perspectives that might be applied. It is not uncommon for a critic to try to explain an ambiguous passage from a novel or poem by citing external factors having to do with social history, psychological theories, logic and philosophy, and/or ethical convictions of the author. Perhaps no discipline offers more opportunities for using the full range of critical perspectives than does literary criticism.

Summary

Reading across the disciplines causes us to make use of all five perspectives, though not always in equal measure. In general, the study of history favors the social perspective, while mathematics and the physical sciences incline toward analytical logic. Social sciences, such as economics and anthropology, often invite a blending of social and logical perspectives. Scholarly studies of the arts and of literature draw us toward the full range of critical perspectives but currently tend to stress rhetorical analysis, otherwise known as the study of form. Literary criticism in recent years has been increasingly concerned with the rhetorical problem of ambiguity. But though separate disciplines may cause us to rely more heavily on some perspectives than on others, no text is exempt from any perspective that the reader wishes to use.

PART THREE

Judging

Chapter 7

The Critic's Role

This book has so far dealt with two of the major stages in critical reading. We've looked at elementary rules for improving comprehension, and we've discussed ways of interpreting a text from several perspectives. The next stage of the critical process is one that some people enjoy and others dread: the act of judgment.

In general, *judgment* means making a decision. With respect to texts, it usually means making a decision about the quality of what you've read. When you have gone beyond interpreting and begun to judge, you will have taken on the role that many people think of when they hear the word "critic."

What Is a Critic?

A critic is sometimes defined as a person who forms and expresses judgments according to certain values. If that is the case, then all of us might be critics. For who among us does not form and express judgments based on values that seem important to us?

Many people think of a critic as someone whose business is to praise or condemn, instead of someone like themselves who engages in the difficult process of applying values. Popular culture may have something to do with that misconception. In today's media, a "critic" can be a sixty-second-spot commentator on TV who rates films and other spectacles numerically or by other simplified means, sometimes with only vague hints as to why a judgment was reached. Not surprisingly, many people think of critics as arbitrary publicists — and of criticism as little more than "hype."

We won't digress into a debate over the role of TV critics, many of whom are intelligent and trustworthy. The point is simply that, in a wider sense, a critic must be more than a score-giver. To reach a judgment we need criteria to use in making up our minds. A responsible critic, whether on television or in print or speaking out in class, needs to make clear what his or her criteria are. In other words, the critic needs to reveal his or her own values as they apply to the object being judged.

What Are Values?

A *value* is a kind of worth which the reader sees as belonging to a text or other object. There are many kinds of values, just as there are many ideas of what is worthwhile. All of us judge according to what we think is valuable, of course, but a given reader is likely to place more emphasis on some values than on others. For example, readers who are greatly concerned with *moral values* may tend to judge favorably texts which uphold the kind of morality they approve of, while condemning ones that do not. Other values include *aesthetic* (or artistic) values, *theoretical* (or logical) values, and *social* (or practical) values having to do with a text's immediate usefulness or cultural relevance. Chances are that your judgment of a text will largely depend on which values concern you most in a given situation.

If you have read Chapter 4 carefully, you should recognize that the range of values you might apply in judging a text is closely related to the range of perspectives that apply when you interpret a text.

For example, if you have looked at a text from a social *perspective*, you will probably find yourself estimating its social *values* when you come to judge it. Those values might include the usefulness of the text as a bearer of practical information. If the text is a newspaper article, college textbook, or book about how to do something, surely you will want to estimate how useful the information is to you or to society at large. If the text is about history, or if it is an imaginative work describing the behavior of characters, you will no doubt have feelings about its value as a guide to history or human behavior. *aesthetically pleasing*

If you've looked at the text from either an emotional or rhetorical perspective, you will probably find yourself gauging what are often called *aesthetic values*. The intensity of your response to a text's images or emotional language will probably lead you to judge how deeply affecting (or perhaps how shallow) the text is emotionally. Your study of the text's rhetoric may cause you to evaluate the form, style, and possible symbolism as being more or less aesthetically appealing.

If you've applied the logical perspective, you may have made up your mind about the *theoretical* values of the text. In contrast to purely social or aesthetic values, theoretical value has to do with issues of truth or falsehood. If you found the text reasonably persuasive in its argument, you might then give it high marks for its theoretical value, whereas if you are left in doubt you might hold it to account for whatever fallacies or misleading conclusions it reached.

Finally, if you have looked at the text from an ethical perspective, you will have touched on the oldest question in value judgment: Are the *ethical* values of the text such that you can respect them even if you can't accept them? In a democratic society we tend to respect each other's differing moral beliefs about what may constitute the highest good. Thus we don't automatically condemn a text just because it seems to uphold ideals different from our own. Nevertheless, we do have a right, indeed a responsibility, to evaluate the convictions a text may have about how its ideals should be achieved. Obviously, it is one thing to believe that happiness is the highest good but quite another to argue that the

ends justify any means for achieving them. It is possible to
respect a text's idealism but have serious reservations about
the actions a text recommends taking. Clearly, you ought to
take your own moral convictions into account in estimating
the ethical value of what you've read.

Thus there are several kinds of values to consider when
you are making up your mind about a text. Those values
often relate to the interpretive perspectives you've used in
making your analysis of what the text says. As you draw comparisons between your values and those of the text, you'll
find that it is possible to discuss strengths and/or weaknesses
in several areas. But chances are that one or a few of those
areas will have the greatest effect on your overall judgment.

How Do Values Apply in the Critical Process?

Values are what lie behind a critic's overall judgment of a
text. If a reader rates a work highly with respect to social
values but low with regard to its aesthetic values (as might
be the case, say, when reading a telegram), the reader's
overall estimate of the text will depend on which of those
values counts most under the circumstances. A textbook
you've read may not have affected you much emotionally or
even ethically, but it might have had considerable value in
terms of its social and theoretical applicability. Thus you
might rate that textbook highly even if it doesn't exactly
"turn you on." Then again, a personal essay that is not
deeply concerned with logic might rate high in terms of its
aesthetic (i.e., emotional and/or rhetorical) values. You are
justified in rewarding those values with praise if you believe
the author's aim was to make you feel strongly about his or
her topic.

Because values are so closely related to critical perspectives, it is often the case that value judgment occurs as part
of interpretation. Rarely will you find a critical essay that
waits until the last line to tell you whether or not the critic
approves of the text. Rather, you'll find value judgments
emerging from the interpretive commentary itself.

Consider, for example, how two different students pass judgment on the essay by Lewis Thomas reprinted in the Appendix. One student, while interpreting the essay from a social perspective, says this:

```
I think Dr. Thomas ignores some very impor-
tant moral issues in his essay.  He points
to some of the terrible by-products of sci-
entific advancement, and then he goes on to
say, trust science.  We have made some mis-
takes, but we are scientists and we will
clean up the mess by more scientific appli-
cation.  It sounds to me as though a doctor
would say, "I gave you a disease but trust
me--I will cure you."
```

It's evident that this student's judgment is affected by social values having to do with the protection of the environment. Rightly or wrongly, he doesn't feel that Thomas has been cautious enough about the threats science can pose to society.

But another student says this:

```
I believe that Lewis Thomas has written a
valuable essay that may convince a reader
uninterested in or even hostile towards the
scientific community.  Research in all its
forms should be supported globally, and
perhaps essays such as this are needed now
and then to focus our attention in this
direction.
```

Here we see a favorable judgment being passed on the basis of other values, mainly theoretical ones. The student prizes the ideal of progress and thinks Thomas has convincingly shown the need for scientific research. She finds the author reflecting his own curiosity about the future of technology, too.

Does the fact that two students pass different judgments based on different values mean that one student is right and the other wrong? Your answer to that question may depend on *your* values. But what we can say for sure is that criticism must involve value judgment to some degree, and that the judgments you reach will have a great deal to do with what you value most.

What Qualifies a Student or General Reader to Be a Critic?

This is a very important question. The answer is based on two assumptions. First, you are qualified to be a critic because you have values of your own that can be applied in making judgments. Second, it is a principle of democracy that each person is entitled to express his or her own ideas.

Often students and general readers are reluctant to think of themselves as "critics." There is a modesty that inclines them to suppose that the role should belong to someone else. A "real" critic, many people feel, is a professional whose experience and expertise qualify him or her to form and express judgments. The rest of us, according to this line of thinking, are amateurs who should keep our mouths shut, take notes, and believe what the experts tell us.

There is, of course, some truth in the view that scholars and other learned critics bring more expertise to their criticism than do those of us who are less experienced; and certainly we should be prepared to listen to the opinions of experts. But it does not follow that our own opinions don't count or that we have no right as general readers to express judgments about what we read. Because each reader is different, bringing separate experiences and emotions to a text, no *one* reader can speak for everyone else. The role of the critic is not to dictate what others must believe, but to speak for oneself as an individual reader.

What we're really getting at here is *freedom of speech.* Exercising that freedom is important if we are to avoid los-ing it. The First Amendment of the U.S. Constitution says this:

> Congress shall make no law respecting an establishment of religion, or prohibiting the free exercise thereof; or abridging the freedom of speech or of the press; or the right of the people peaceably to assemble, and to petition the Government for a redress of grievances.

If you want to know what qualifies you to be a critic, look closely at those words. They guarantee you the right to believe, read, say, write, and ask for whatever you want. And if you're doing all those things freely, you are applying values and reaching judgments of your own. That is what criticism is all about. The Constitution, not a diploma, is your license to be a critic.

Why Do Critics Disagree?

Anyone who participates in critical discussions or who reads book reviews knows that critics disagree. To paraphrase an old saying, "One reader's meat is another's poison." The judgment that you form about a text may bring you into conflict with someone else's judgment; and even if it seems that everyone is praising or condemning a given text, you're bound to find a dissenter if you look far enough. Maybe that dissenter is you!

The reason that critics disagree is that values differ among individuals. Earlier in this chapter we saw how two students pass differing judgments on Lewis Thomas's "Making Science Work," one student having been influenced by his own social values, the other by her own theoretical values. For those two students to reach an agreement, one of them would have to change not only his or her view of the essay, but also his or her own value system. That's not likely to happen, at least on the spur of the moment.

Criticism resembles politics. Some thinkers even believe that criticism *is* politics, insofar as many of the same factors go into evaluating a text as go into deciding whether or not to support a candidate. Does the text (or candidate) represent your own values? Does the text (or candidate) inspire your trust? Does the text (or candidate) deserve to win popular approval? Do you *like* what the text (or candidate) is saying? Whatever your response to those questions may be in a given circumstance, you can bet that not everyone will share your judgment. No text (or candidate) ever gets a hundred percent of the votes. Not everyone agrees that the best text (or candidate) has won popular approval. And, in fact, not everyone is willing to vote.

However, reading is a far more individualized matter than is a political campaign. The important question is not what everyone else thinks about a text, or whether or not a text "wins" approval in the public arena, but rather what *you* think of the text as a result of your experiences with it. Nevertheless, when you openly declare your judgment — whether in oral discussion or in writing — you are going public with your ideas. At that point it may actually be helpful to think of yourself as a politician of sorts, ready for the heat and struggle of the campaign. If what you say wins some agreement from others, you'll gain confidence in your own judgment. But be ready, too, for the jibes and rebuttals from those who see things differently. Be ready — but don't be resentful. Remember that disagreement is a normal part of the critic's role.

Summary

The act of judgment results from an interpretation of the text. Although many people think of a critic as someone who praises or condemns, the role of the critic as judge is to apply personal values. All readers are entitled to judge what they read, but a responsible critic makes clear what the basis of his or her judgment is. Because values differ among individuals, we must regard disagreement as a normal part of critical discussion.

Chapter 8

Judging by Values
You Respect

Let us consider how times and values change.

About two hundred years ago the most powerful critic in the Western world was a Scottish lawyer named Francis Jeffrey. As a contributor to the famous *Edinburgh Review*, he wrote articles about new authors, recommending or dis-recommending their works to the English-speaking public of Europe and America. Lord Jeffrey was a learned man with a strong sense of social values. He believed that his judgment of a book should reflect the "universal" interests common to "whole classes of persons" rather than "peculiar" interests which only a few individuals might share. Consistent with what he thought were universal social values, Jeffrey proceeded to write hostile reviews of Romantic authors whose works seemed to him peculiar or intended only for a few sensitive minds. He is now remembered, if at all, for the opening line of a review he wrote about the poetry of William Wordsworth, declaring "This will never do!"

Wordsworth eventually acquired fame despite Jeffrey's judgment, and hardly anyone now remembers who the Scottish reviewer was. But even if it now seems that a critic who condemned Wordsworth must have been a fool, it's also clear that Jeffrey was judging by values which he and many of his contemporaries respected. Moreover, if values had not gradually changed in the public world that Lord

Jeffrey sought to advise, we probably wouldn't find poems by
Wordsworth on the reading lists of college literature courses
today. It took a new set of values and a new court of critics
to reverse the Scotsman's judgment, and it took growing respect for those newer values and critics to change public
opinion.

The critic is always at risk. Even if everyone seems to
agree with your judgment at the moment, there's no telling
what forces may overrule you in the future. Each of us risks
becoming another Francis Jeffrey the second we declare that
a given text will or will not do. But at least we can judge
by values we respect, knowing that whatever happens we've
been true to ourselves. We can only hope that we've also
been true to the text.

How Do Values Change over Time?

If we look at history, we see that certain values seem more
popular in some periods than in others. It's true that human
consciousness has always been concerned with social, aesthetic, theoretical, and moral values. But like fashion, the
history of value judgment reveals a series of passing vogues.

A survey of how fashions have changed in English criticism over the past five hundred years might be summarized
as follows. In the Renaissance, we find powerful critics such
as Francis Bacon and Philip Sidney trying to bring together
the theoretical virtues of logic and the aesthetic values of
art. The aim was to encourage what Sidney called "sweet
food of sweetly uttered knowledge." Later, however, many
seventeenth-century authors seemed more concerned with
reconciling the theoretical values of logic with the moral
values of religion. Later still, in the Romantic period of the
late eighteenth and early nineteenth centuries, a vogue of
emotional intensity sought to raise aesthetic values to new
heights. In the Victorian period that followed, moral values
reasserted themselves widely in critical discourse. But toward
the end of the nineteenth century, there was a revolt by
some influential critics in favor of pure aestheticism — or "art

for art's sake." To view art as something separate from morality is the essence of aestheticism, but "art for art's sake" also implies intense interest in rhetorical form, or *how* a work is composed. That concern marks the beginning, at least, of critical fashion in our own century. Within the past ninety years, however, the spectrum of critical values has changed again, and now the possibilities seem wider than ever before.

The twentieth century is remarkable for the diversity of its critical methods and the wide range of values that critics apply. The multiplying of educational fields, the growth of communications media, and the subsequent broadening of international cultural awareness have led to an enrichment of critical discussion, but also, some say, to a situation in which no clear value system can prevail. Today we have critics specializing in social analysis, psychological analysis, rhetorical and logical analysis, ethical analysis, and dozens of hybrid combinations. The values that those approaches entail are sometimes at odds with each other, creating what to some may seem like a critical gridlock — a rush-hour traffic jam where so many books, articles, and lectures clog the academic thoroughfares that it's hard to see where we're going. But this situation may be more beneficial than it seems.

What Is the Benefit of Diversity?

There may be an element of truth in the complaint that critical diversity has led to a sense of disorder — or to "future shock." But there is also this. We have lived in a century when respect for each individual's opinions and values has been advanced. If we look back a hundred or more years, we find plenty of thunderous voices trying to pass judgment on behalf of entire societies by identifying, as the Victorian critic Matthew Arnold said, "the best that has been known and said in the world." Now that kind of grand presumption may be no longer possible. In a century that has turned with so much interest to its own cultural diversity, adjectives like "best" and "worst" are increasingly hard to justify. As the modern French critic Roland Barthes put it in the 1970s: "the text (the same is true of the singing voice) can wring from me only this judgment, in no way adjectival: *that's it*! And further still: *that's it for me!*"

In a time when you are free to express your own values, the problem becomes whether you are true to yourself when you say "That's it for me!" Passing judgment is easy if any values will do. But to judge by values you respect may call for personal courage as you face disagreement from people who do not share those values. If the main benefit of diversity is freedom, the main burden is having to speak for yourself.

Are Values Absolute?

One reason why various kinds of values seem to ascend or descend in critical popularity over the centuries may be the unresolved question of whether values themselves are absolute or relative. If, as many idealists believe, there are some transcendent values known to the human heart but imperfectly reflected in reality, we might try to intuit an absolute order of values. But if, as held by some pragmatic thinkers of our own times and earlier, values are contingent on the social and economic forces within a particular society at a given time in history, we may be led to conclude that values are not absolute — but uncertain and pluralistic. The absolutists have on their side the evidence that some authors — such as Homer and Shakespeare — have survived in esteem throughout the centuries, as have human aspirations toward goodness, truth, and beauty. The relativists have on their side the evidence that authors, including Homer and Shakespeare, have been evaluated by different criteria at different times, and that ideas of what is good, true, or beautiful vary widely from one generation to another and between cultures.

As this debate continues, so does the argument over how best to assert one's judgment of a text. The absolutist might advise looking for evidence of universal social value, transcendent beauty, eternal truths revealed by logic, and the highest moral good. A relativist might say that it is important to consider what you find socially useful given your present circumstances, what feelings you have at the moment, what seems reasonable to you now, and whether or not what is good for the text is good for you and the society around you.

The question of whether values are absolute or relative may also affect how you view the certainty of your own critical judgments. You may be led to ask whether the values you respect now are timeless and permanent or simply the reflection of your changing life. The controversy over this issue is very old. It is bound to continue.

Conclusion

As readers we are of course free to choose sides in the debate over the nature of values, just as we are free to set priorities as to which values matter most in our overall estimate of a text's quality. We are even free *not* to judge, relying instead on interpretation alone to serve as the dynamic and always unfinished guide to what a text has meant or may come to mean. But if we do judge, surely the judgment should not be an act of impulse. Rather, it should be the result of an interpretive process that takes into account the many kinds of values that a text — any text — can offer to the careful reader.

After all, texts are not people. But they are of people and, as such, complex and often difficult to understand. They have about them the assertiveness, the insecurities, the emotive charms and calculated manners of life, not to mention their own ways of reasoning and believing. In some respects they are even more vulnerable than people, being dependent entirely on your sensitivity and compassion. Each text comes alone to your hands. It speaks to you persistently in a tone of its own. It shares your space. You may choose it freely or reject it for another. The text has no choice. You are its reader, the one it must please.

PART FOUR

Writing

Chapter 9

Forms of Written Response

Writing relates to reading in much the same way that speaking relates to listening. As children we learned to talk by hearing and responding to what our parents and other people said. As we grew older, our involvement in conversations strengthened our vocabulary, determined our accents and tone of voice, and made us participants in the oral communication process of an adult world. Similarly, the act of reading can make us active participants in written language. That means responding to texts with writing of our own.

Though it's possible to limit your response to oral remarks or "thinking out loud," the process of reading leads ultimately to the act of writing, not merely to speech alone. And it is by writing in response to reading that you can learn and remember most about the language of the text.

There are many possible forms of written response. This chapter is concerned with those which college students and general readers may find most useful: notes, diaries, and essays.

Notes

You'll find that notes are the simplest kind of written response. They are brief reminders of what you find important, interesting, or questionable about the material you're reading. There are basically two kinds of notes that you can make: page annotations and research notes.

What Are Page Annotations?

Page annotations are comments that you write in the margins of whatever text you are reading. It goes without saying that in order to take notes of this kind, you must first *own* the text. Marking up borrowed library books is a crime punishable by pangs of guilt as well as by other possible sanctions.

Annotating is a practice that goes back to medieval times when monks wrote *glosses* in the margins of religious manuscripts. One purpose of a gloss — or annotation — was to cross-reference one part of a book with another part to indicate where a topic or theme was developed or repeated. You can still do that kind of cross-referencing if you put in marginal notes such as "See also page 32" to remind yourself where to refer. But modern indexes, which usually appear at the backs of nonfiction books, have eliminated the need for most cross-referencing by hand, except of course in the case of fiction and other genres which do not carry indexes.

Probably the most useful kinds of annotations to make are those which call attention to key passages which you sense are worth remembering for review. For example, if a page contains a *definition* of a special term or a *conclusion* about some issue, you'll probably want to mark the place with a note of your own. Also, when you come across a term or sentence that seems arguable or ambiguous, you might want to pose a question in the margin: for example, "What does this mean?" Later you'll have a chance to look up the term in a reference book or to ask an expert.

In short, there are many ways of annotating a page, as well as many reasons for doing so. In Figure 1 you see an example of an annotated page from Lewis Thomas's *Late Night Thoughts on Listening to Mahler's Ninth Symphony*, the book in which "Making Science Work" appears. Notice

Figure 1

ing into high gear only within the last fifty years. We have not lacked explanations at any time in our recorded history, but now we must live and think with <u>the new habit of requiring reproducible observations</u> and solid facts for the explanations. It is not as easy a time for us as it used to be: we are raised through childhood in skepticism and disbelief; we feel the need of proofs all around, even for matters as deep as the working of our own consciousness, where there is as yet no clear prospect of proof about anything. <u>Uncertainty,</u> disillusion, and despair are prices to be paid for living in an age of science. <u>Illumination is the product sought,</u> but it comes in small bits, only from time to time, not ever in broad, bright flashes of public comprehension, and there can be no promise that we will ever emerge from the great depths of the mystery of being.

Nevertheless, <u>we have started to do science on a world scale, and to rely on it,</u> and hope for it. Not just the scientists, everyone, and not for the hope of illumination, but for the sure predictable

def. of scientific method

\!

See p. 19

(continued)

Figure 1 (continued)

prospect of new technologies, which have always come along, like spray in the wake of science. <u>We need better ways of predicting how a piece of new technology is likely to turn out,</u> better measures available on an international level to shut off the ones that carry hazard to the life of the planet (including, but perhaps not always so much *first of all,* as is usually the only consideration, our own species' life). <u>We will have to go more warily</u> with technology in the future, for the demands will be increasing and the stakes will be very high. Instead of coping, or trying to cope, with the wants of four billion people, we will very soon be facing the needs, probably desperate, of double that number and, soon thereafter, double again.

How can we do this?

that the annotations include a cross-reference, a note calling attention to the author's definition of scientific method, and a response question from the reader. Your own annotating of this page might include other sorts of remarks or questions.

What Are Research Notes?

Research notes are records which you keep on index cards. While you must own a text in order to make page annotations, you can take research notes whenever you are reading borrowed material. The great advantage of such notes is that you can assemble and rearrange them easily if you plan to write an essay involving quoted material.

There are basically two ways of taking research notes. The first is to record *direct quotations* from the text, including the page number, to show where you are copying from. Direct quotations are word-for-word transcribings of what an author says, and you should be careful to put quotation marks (" ") around each copied passage. Obviously, you will want to include in your research notes only those direct quotations that seem especially important to you.

The second kind of research note is a *summary*, or brief paraphrase in your own words, of some part of the text. Here again, you'll want to record the page number(s) of the part you are summarizing, especially if you plan on citing the text in a research paper. Summarizing is often useful when you need to make a brief record of an author's argument or to remind yourself of his or her main train of thought.

Research notes may become the basis for future research papers, or they can serve simply as a record of your reading. On the chance that the text you're noting will have to be cited in a formal report, you should always make sure that the first note card you fill out includes publishing information needed for listing on a bibliography page. In the case of a book, that means writing down the following information: author(s), title, edition number (if not the first), city of publication, publishing house, and date of the edition (usually found on the back of the title page). In the case of articles, it usually means writing down the name of the author, the name of the article, the name of the newspaper or magazine, the date of the issue, and the numbers of the first and last pages of the article. Even more information may be needed if you are dealing with an anthology or collection of works by separate authors.

Figure 2 shows two note cards. The first illustrates a direct quotation from a book, the second a brief summary from a magazine article.

Figure 2

```
Brownmiller, Susan.  Femininity.
  New York: Linden-Simon, 1984.

"A powerful esthetic that is built upon a
recognition of powerlessness is a slip-
pery subject to grapple with, for its
contradictions are elusive, ephemeral and
ultimately impressive."

                                      (19)
```

```
Roth, Philip.  "A Conversation in
Prague."
  The New York Review of Books
  12 April 1990: 14-22.

An interview between Roth and Czech
writer Ivan Klíma.  Discussion covers re-
cent literary history of Czechoslovakia,
with special focus on authors Franz Kafka
(19-20), Milan Kundera (16-17), and
Václav Havel (20-21).
```

Diaries

A diary is a record of your own experiences. To "keep a
diary" means jotting down information daily in a private
notebook. What you jot down may include comments on
events, people, places, and (very important for our purposes)
things you've read. There have been many famous diaries in

history, such as those kept by Samuel Pepys, André Gide, and Anais Nin. But for most people keeping a diary remains a private and unshared enterprise. Actually, a diary is a way of building an autobiography — a story of your life. Part of that life is bound to be spent reading.

What Is a Reader's Diary?

A reader's diary is simply a diary that pays fairly close attention to what you're reading from day to day. There's no rule that says the same diary can't include other subjects, too — including events, weather, worries, or whatever else. But as a form of written response, the diary should become a record of your life as a reader. You should be able to look back at the pages after a few months or years and be reminded of what you were reading today.

Why Keep That Sort of Diary?

Unlike annotating pages or taking research notes, keeping a diary allows you to focus on the circumstances in which reading takes place, as well as on your responses to texts. Although you may find yourself recording some quotations, much as you would on index cards, a diary gives you the chance to record such matters as the day, the setting, and the reasons you came to read a particular text.

Keeping a diary can make you aware of your reading habits and preferences. It can reveal to you how your education is developing. But most of all, a diary has the advantage of personalizing your reading in a way that note taking alone cannot do. As you record things in a diary, you come to realize that what you've read, like the places and people you've encountered, is very much a part of your own life story.

Are There Special Guidelines for Keeping a Diary?

No. A diary is a private form, and how you choose to comment privately is your own business. Some diarists like to do

a good deal of quoting so that they'll be able to refer to the
diary as a source book in the future. Others like to concentrate on their own responses to texts, perhaps commenting
from one or more critical perspectives we've discussed earlier. If a text you have just read seems important for social,
emotional, rhetorical, logical, and/or ethical reasons, you
might jot down some thoughts as to why. But no matter
what you choose to say, the diary should be a working re-
minder of your life as a reader.

Here, for example, is a sample page from a reader's diary.
You'll notice that the information included probably means
more to the diary keeper than it would mean to anyone else:

April 25th

All the ice on Lake Mendota has now melted, and this
morning I tossed crumbs to the ducks. This week I have two
chapters for Economics, and Friday there will be a test on
Janson's book in Art History. I'm trying to finish a paper for
English by the end of the month, but I'm not yet to the
proofreading stage. In *The Elements of Style* E. B. White
says, "Style takes its final shape more from attitudes of mind
than from principles of composition. . . ." I agree with his
view of rhetoric, and I hope my professor feels the same way!

In the afternoon I waited for Emma on the student-union
terrace. She was late, so I passed the time by reading the
newspaper someone had left. It was full of reports from East-
ern Europe. Emma arrived just as I was finishing an article
on *perestroika*. I looked up and saw her smiling. She was
wearing old jeans and a sweatshirt, and beyond her shoulder
there were sailboats on the lake.

Critical Essays

The third and best known kind of written response is the
critical essay. Here you go beyond page annotating or diary
keeping. The aim is to develop a prose composition about
the text you've read. Students in college may be asked to
write this sort of essay as part of their course work, while

specialists within various disciplines often write critical essays to be published as book reviews. In general, a critical essay may be classified as either a *personal response essay* or a *critical research essay*, depending on whether or not the writer uses library resources to help develop the discussion.

What Is a Personal Response Essay?

As the name implies, a personal response essay emphasizes direct response to the text. Aside from your own feelings, thoughts, and chosen critical perspective, the only source for the paper will be the text you are writing about. A personal response essay does not involve doing library research or consulting other outside sources. What you report in the paper is entirely the result of your own thinking about the text.

Normally, the development of a personal response essay follows the critical process we've reviewed earlier in this book. After reading a text carefully, interpreting it from one or more of the major perspectives, and reaching an evaluative judgment, you should be ready to begin writing. If you're not, you might consider some of the guidelines discussed in Chapter 10.

The following is an example of a short personal response essay written by a student. In this case the text under discussion is Joan Didion's "On Going Home" (see the Appendix). The student's essay blends social, emotional, and rhetorical perspectives, but the overall response is very much the writer's own.

A COMMENTARY ON DIDION'S
"ON GOING HOME"

by

Mary Jane Quinn

On returning home for her daughter's birthday, Joan Didion feels pulled in two directions. One is toward the insular con-

fines of her family, the other toward her
new life in L.A. Her experience is one
shared by many people. Going home is both
painful and comforting--the small child
within feels both threatened and safe.

The author rediscovers objects of emotional significance: "A bathing suit I wore
the summer I was seventeen. A letter of
rejection from The Nation. . . . Three
teacups hand-painted with cabbage roses and
signed 'E.M.,' my grandmother's initials."
These mementoes from the author's past
can't be disposed of. They represent more
than memories; they define her.

If there is any motive it may be just
one of understanding, of sorting out all
the conflicting feelings evoked by a visit
home. At the end of the essay she speaks
of her daughter, open and trusting, of
wanting to give her a sense of family and
home, but knowing that their lives are
different and that she can't make those
promises.

I think Didion's essay is valuable because it describes a very real conflict
that many people may feel. Returning home
as an adult, especially with children of
your own, can be a bittersweet experience.
It is difficult for most people not to fall
into old patterns, assuming the role of a
child once more in your parents' home.
Didion's essay does a sensitive job of
exploring those emotions, ones that are

at times not completely understood by
ourselves.

You will notice that in the preceding paper the student has
relied on her own interests and convictions to interpret Didion's essay. The main line of development in this case favors
the emotional perspective because it is from that viewpoint
that the student finds Didion's work most intriguing. However, the student has also commented in passing on the social and rhetorical aspects of the text. Although no outside
sources (apart from Didion's essay) are directly involved, the
student does quote from the text and alludes to specific details mentioned by Didion. Quotations and allusion serve to
clarify the student's interpretive analysis and to support her
favorable evaluation of the text.

What Is a Critical Research Essay?

Like the personal response essay, the critical research essay
records your own interpretation of a text. The only major
difference is that a research essay does involve using library
resources as part of your report. Although the main thrust of
the essay must remain your own response to the text, here
you expand the discussion somewhat by quoting what other
authorities have to say.

Finding secondary sources related to your topic usually
means spending some hours at the library. To save time,
you should have an idea of what you're searching for. One
way of narrowing your search and saving time is to let
yourself be guided by the critical perspective you're most
interested in. For example, let's say you've decided to write
from a social perspective on Lewis Thomas's essay "Making
Science Work." Once you'd found out (say, from an anthology note) that the essay was contained in Thomas's
book *Late Night Thoughts on Listening to Mahler's Ninth
Symphony* (1983), you could locate that book and read the
rest of it in search of other essays that bore on social issues

related to science. Often the most useful secondary sources
are works by the same author.

Also, you might search the library's card catalog or data
base for books by other authors relating to the history of
science in the twentieth century. Perhaps you might find
contrasting remarks from other writers on how science has
affected our society.

Still another possibility is to look for book reviews in
which critics have discussed and evaluated Thomas's book.
General indexes such as *Book Review Digest* could help you
find the newspapers and magazines in which those reviews
appear. By reading and preparing to quote critical remarks
other than your own, you can give your research report a
wider scope and perhaps learn more about the significance
of the text.

Students sometimes fear that they won't be able to find
any "outside sources," but the problem is more often of an
opposite kind: there are so *many* possible sources (i.e., works
by the same author, by other authors in the same field,
as well as book reviews, etc.) that you're likely to feel
swamped. The great danger of research is not that you won't
turn up anything, but that you'll turn up so much that your
own response to the text will get lost in the shuffle of note
cards. That is why it's a good idea to start your project by
writing a personal response essay *first*, then gradually expand
that personal essay into a research essay by adding quotations from other sources as they seem appropriate.

The following paper is a slightly condensed version of
a student's critical research paper on Lewis Thomas. The
writer has taken what is mainly a rhetorical perspective,
though he also makes use of social and emotional viewpoints on the text. You'll notice that he has expanded the
topic to include not only "Making Science Work," but also
other essays from Thomas's *Late Night Thoughts*. This student has chosen to quote a number of book reviews as well.
In citing those secondary sources, he has followed a standard
documentation procedure explained in most English composition handbooks (see also Chapter 10).

LEWIS THOMAS: "MAKING SCIENCE WORK" AND MAKING IT MORE HUMAN

by

Brian Wilson

Although Lewis Thomas usually writes about science and includes many scientific facts in his essays, it would be wrong to think that he writes mainly in order to teach science. Thomas's writings show the connections between the world of science and society as a whole. Readers are made to feel that they can relate to science and so become more accepting of Thomas's explicit arguments that scientific research should be pursued vigorously. In order to make people feel positive about science, Thomas must fight against the negative image that many people hold of science. One reason that so many people feel alienated from science is the technical and impersonal way that it is reported. As Martin Washburn puts it:

. . . what I have always loathed about science is not its content but its chosen style. At the level at which ordinary citizens experience it, the message of science has been that emotional alienation and objectivity are the same (check out the decor in your doctor's or dentist's office). (33)

But Thomas immediately puts readers at ease
with his "chatty, aware, and charmingly
civilized" style (Washburn 33). Thomas
portrays science in a very personal way,
giving an emotional response to almost
every scientific fact he mentions:

> The rings of Saturn are the latest sur-
> prise. All my physicist friends are en-
> chanted by this phenomenon, marvelling at
> the small violations of the laws of plan-
> etary mechanics, shocked by the unaccount-
> able braids and spokes stuck there among
> the rings like graffiti. ("The Corner of
> the Eye" 16)

Readers can relate to the excitement and
fun expressed here, without understanding
the physics involved.
     Although scientific work is very com-
plex and precise, Thomas portrays it as a
thoroughly human enterprise:

> Science began by fumbling. It works be-
> cause the people involved in it work, and
> <u>work together</u>. They become excited and
> exasperated, they exchange their bits of
> information at a full shout, and, the most
> wonderful thing of all, they keep <u>at</u> one
> another. ("Alchemy" 33)

Science is shown to be like many other
fields of work; it is done by people who
are emotionally involved and care deeply
about their work.

Thomas does more than just make people feel connected to science the way that wildlife films make people feel connected to the wilderness. His writings inspire wider reflections on science and its relation to other aspects of society, especially politics, philosophy, and music. Jonathan Yardley reviews Thomas's writings this way:

> These [topics] are the concerns of a man who is both a scientist and a humanist, whose essays are trenchant and sometimes moving demonstrations that the two are not mutually exclusive. This is not to say, as is sometimes incorrectly claimed on Thomas's behalf, that he clarifies science for the lay reader. . . . Rather it is to say that Thomas understands, as do too few on either side, that the worlds of the scientist and the humanist should be friendly rather than hostile, that each has much to teach the other, that neither can be completely healthy in smug, self-absorbed isolation. (3)

And according to Joyce Carol Oates, Thomas's essays "insist upon the interrelatedness of all life, . . . [to show that] science cannot be divorced from the rest of our civilization, any more than an individual scientist can be divorced from his participation in the world as a human being." (3)

One way that Thomas relates science to
other aspects of society is to create vivid
images based on scientific research, which
in turn evoke philosophical ideas. For
example, in "The Corner of the Eye," Thomas
writes:

> . . . it was a disappointment not to find
> evidences of life [on Mars], and there was
> some sadness in the pictures sent back to
> earth from the Mars Lander, that lonely
> long-legged apparatus poking about with its
> jointed arm, picking up sample after sample
> of the barren Mars soil, looking for any
> flicker of life and finding none; the only
> sign of life on Mars was the Lander itself,
> an extension of the human mind all the way
> from earth to Mars, totally alone. (16)

This imagery evokes feelings of pride in
man's technological quest to find out about
the universe, but it also makes the reader
appreciate the earth, for this is the only
place that we know of where life exists.

A second way that Thomas connects science to society is to show that scientific
concepts can be used to understand many
other areas of human interest. For example, human emotions and behavior are
studied in the social sciences, which
Thomas believes "may be the most important
scientific business of all":

> Our behavior toward each other is the
> strangest, most unpredictable, and almost

entirely unaccountable of all the phenomena
with which we are obliged to live. In all
of nature there is nothing so threatening
to humanity as humanity itself. ("Making
Science Work" 23)

Thomas also uses scientific concepts as
metaphors for other subjects. This forces
readers to think of scientific concepts out
of their normal context. For example, in
"Making Science Work" he uses scientific
concepts from biology as metaphors for concepts in other areas of science when he
describes the computer networks as being
formed as "interconnected ganglia around
the earth" (22) and compares seismographic
instruments to "medicine's CAT scanners"
(23). This use of scientific terms in
analogies implies that the terms are generally understood by the readers, that science is a part of everyone's life.

Finally, Thomas also shows that the
aims of science are not restricted to triv-
ial concerns or even to the production of
new technological products:

As we learn more about the fundamental processes of living things in general we will
learn more about ourselves, including
perhaps the ways in which our brains . . .
achieve the earth's awareness of itself.
It may be too much to say that we will become wise through such endeavors, but we
can at least come into possession of a

level of information upon which a new kind of wisdom might be based. ("Making Science Work" 20-21)

Lewis Thomas believes that scientific discovery helps to lift humankind to a higher level and opens up new possibilities for us. His belief leads Joyce Carol Oates to conclude that "Dr. Thomas's underlying thesis is certainly a positive and optimistic one. . . . ." (3)

WORKS CITED

Oates, Joyce Carol. "Beyond Common Sense." Rev. of The Lives of a Cell, by Lewis Thomas. The New York Times Book Review 26 May 1974: 2-3.

Thomas, Lewis. "Alchemy." Late Night Thoughts 29-34.

---. Late Night Thoughts on Listening to Mahler's Ninth Symphony. New York: Viking, 1983.

---. "Making Science Work." Late Night Thoughts 18-28.

---. "The Corner of the Eye." Late Night Thoughts 12-17.

Washburn, Martin. Rev. of The Lives of a Cell, by Lewis Thomas. The Village Voice 27 June 1974: 32-33.

Yardley, Jonathan. "Lewis Thomas: A Doctor of Humane Letters." Rev. of Late Night Thoughts on Listening to Mahler's Ninth

Symphony, by Lewis Thomas. Washington
Post Book World 13 Nov. 1983: 3+.

The preceding paper illustrates one student's way of developing a critical research essay. You should know that there are many other ways depending on the text, the perspectives, the kinds of available secondary sources, and above all, your own response to what you've read. It is worth noting, however, that the preceding paper does show how quoted sources can be incorporated into a research essay. By using phrases such as "According to . . . ," the writer has carefully distinguished between his views and those of his sources. Also, though he gives the last word to Joyce Carol Oates, the student himself controls the argument, the organization, and the overall development of the paper. As in the case of a personal response essay, this critical research essay remains an expression of the writer's own views. The difference is that here other sources have been included to add interest and to acknowledge the opinions of other readers.

Summary

The forms of written response include notes, diaries, and critical essays. Making page annotations as part of the reading process can help you study and review texts. Research notes kept on index cards are useful as a means of summarizing borrowed material and gathering quotes. Diaries allow for personal record keeping and help you to be aware of the part that reading plays in your life. Personal response essays, as well as critical research essays, are formal demonstrations of your critical-reading skills.

Chapter 10

Guidelines for Composition

Contrary to what some people think, there is no all-purpose formula for writing criticism. Like other forms of writing, critical discussion is an art that allows for many styles and methods. It would be pointless and dishonest to imply that there is any foolproof system that covers all the possibilities. Nevertheless, we shall conclude this book with a few guidelines — you might say tips — that generally apply to writing from sources.

Discover What You Think

Like reading, the act of writing is a process of discovery. When you are assigned to write about a text you've read, you immediately face the problem of finding something original to say, something that is "your own thinking" and not someone else's. At this point skepticism may set in. You may feel that everything worth saying has already been said — and said by somebody who's a professional or a genius or at least getting an A in the course. If that's true, why not just look up the views of some distinguished critic or other authority, paraphrase what that person said, and just say you agree?

Imitation may be a sincere form of flattery, but it's not often a sincere form of critical thinking. You need to discover what *you* think, and by that discovery form the basis

for agreeing or disagreeing with what previous critics have
said about a text.

Much of this book has already been concerned with how
to discover what you think about a text. But just to review,
let's summarize what's usually involved. First, you should
read the text carefully, paying attention to its organizational
features, the time it was written, its genre, its apparent aims,
its tone of voice, its contrasts, its "heart" (so to speak), and
whatever seems missing. Second, you should reconsider the
text from several perspectives, answering some or all of the
questions that each perspective raises. As you look back at
the text from social, emotional, rhetorical, logical, and ethical viewpoints, you should begin to sense which of those
perspectives concern you most or which enliven your curiosity. Third, you should evaluate the text according to values — social, aesthetic, moral — which you respect. Once
you've gone through that entire process of critical reflection,
you should have a pretty fair idea of where you stand in
relation to the text. Or, to put it another way, you should
have begun to discover what *you* think.

However, the process of discovery continues as you begin
to write. If you have made page annotations or research
notes as described in Chapter 9, you will already have begun sorting out key impressions or points worth stressing.
But when you get to the point of developing an essay, you
will need to put your ideas into a coherent framework, ex-
panding on some matters and subordinating others.

There are several techniques for planning an expanded
essay, but all of them rely on your first acquiring a viewpoint (or combination of perspectives) from which to proceed.
One way to get started on an essay is to use the *question/
answer* technique. You simply pose questions and then
sketch out how you might answer them. Later, in the second draft, you might choose to give more development to
some of those answers than to others. If you refer back to
Chapter 4, you'll see many questions that can be asked
about any text. It's probable that still more questions will
occur to you, depending on the nature of your topic. Some-

times you find that asking one question leads to other questions, until pretty soon you're on your way. Question/answer technique is especially helpful in situations where you are shy about asserting yourself in writing. Many of us are reluctant to start declaring our ideas flatly, but few of us have trouble forming some kind of answer once a question has been asked.

Another way to get started is to use a technique called *brainstorming*. In practice that usually means jotting some lists of terms which occur to you as you apply your critical perspective or perspectives. Here, for example, are a couple of "brainstorm" lists that a student might draw up using the social and rhetorical perspectives on the Gettysburg Address:

Social	*Rhetorical*
Civil War	Speech
Ceremony	Contrast
Battlefield	Sentence length
Dedication	Repetition
Audience	Parallelism
Democracy	Personification
Etc.	Etc.

Once you have made some "brainstorm" lists, you can proceed to choose terms that interest you for further development as subtopics. Chances are that you won't use every term you've listed, but some will prove useful as a guide to what your written discussion will be about.

A useful variant of the brainstorming technique is to draw up lists of contrasts which you see as central to the structure of the text you're writing about. Here is an example of such a list pertaining to Lincoln's speech:

past/present

dead/living

task behind/task ahead

slavery/freedom

others/ourselves

then/now

It's easy to see that by developing comments on these binary oppositions you would soon find yourself applying one or more critical perspectives automatically. The contrast of past/present, for example, could involve the social, rhetorical, and ethical perspectives, depending on your critical viewpoint.

There are several other techniques for getting started and discovering what you think. One of them is called *clustering*, a practice similar to brainstorm listing, except that you write terms and ideas around a circle drawn on a piece of paper. Another is known simply as *free writing*, or in other words writing fast and without stopping for a specified period of time (let's say twenty minutes), without worrying about form but letting one sentence lead to another in a process of rapid association. Free writing can help you overcome "writer's block" and give you at least something on paper to rework. Finally, there is the time-honored method called *outlining*, by which you arrange your ideas in a formal order according to numbers and letters (I./A./1.2./B.1.2.3./C. etc.), usually in a vertical format. Outlines can be brief and sketchy or elaborately detailed, but their chief value is to let you study the topic sequence of your writing and the proportions of the whole composition. Formal outlining often works best as a follow-up to one or more of the other planning techniques.

However you begin to work on a composition, remember too that writing always involves rewriting (i.e., redrafting, editing, and proofreading). Rewriting takes time, of course, but doing it continues the process of discovering what you think.

Use the Text for Evidence

A common problem in student and amateur writing is vagueness, also known as unsupported generalization. It is often tempting to write sweeping statements about a topic without providing examples to show or prove what you mean. But to be convincing you must demonstrate the validity of your analysis by supplying evidence. In science, evidence takes the form of data drawn from experiments. In literary and critical studies, evidence usually takes the form of quotations drawn from the text or texts being discussed.

To learn how quotations work as evidence, you might spend some time reading scholarly book reviews, most of which contain plenty of quotes to support the reviewer's analysis. Here, for example, is a brief excerpt from a professional review of *The Collected Letters of W. B. Yeats*, vol. 1 (Oxford: Clarendon, 1986). Yeats was a great Irish poet who lived during the late nineteenth and early twentieth centuries. The reviewer, Professor Denis Donoghue, is bringing an emotional perspective to bear on Yeats's early writings:

> Yeats wavered between . . . two moods. When he was immersed in esoteric lore, he trusted to the strength of the poetic tradition he avowed. Sometimes, as in a letter of December 21, 1888, to Katharine Tynan, he thought the procedure too much of a good thing:

> > We both of us need to substitute more and more the landscapes of nature for the landscapes of Art. I myself have another and kindred need — to substitute the feelings and longings of nature for those of art . . . We should make poems on the familar landscapes we love not the strange and rare and glittering scenes we wonder at — these latter are the landscapes of Art, the rouge of nature.

> But there were still other times when Yeats thought — it is a nuance of the first mood — that what mattered was not the objects in view but the suspension of one's will in their presence. In "Symbolism in Painting" (1898) he wrote:

> > A person or a landscape that is a part of a story or a portrait evokes but so much emotion as the story or the portrait can permit without loosening the bonds that make it a story or a portrait; but if you liberate a person or a landscape from the bonds of motives and their actions, causes and their effects, and from all bonds but the bonds of your love, it will change under your eyes, and become a symbol of an infinite emotion, a perfected emotion, a part of the Divine Essence; for we love nothing but the perfect, and our dreams make all things perfect, that we may love them.

In later words, "the mind liberated from the pressure of the
will is unfolded in symbols."

—from "The Young Yeats,"
The New York Review of Books
14 Aug. 1986: 14–16

Notice that here the critic illustrates his thesis about Yeats's
"moods" by quoting from three sources (one from the book
being reviewed and the others from Yeats's later writings).
The quotes serve to illustrate the poet's longing for nature
on the one hand and his love of symbolic dreams on the
other. Without the quotes for evidence, we might have trouble believing or even understanding the point about Yeats's
moods. But given the evidence, we have reason to find Professor Donoghue's analysis convincing.

The kinds and sources of quotations you use for evidence
may depend on a variety of factors, such as what you're
trying to show, how much you've read about a subject, and
of course your critical perspective on the material. Scholars
with years of experience in a given field may have an easier
time locating useful quotes from a range of sources than will
a relatively inexperienced writer. But even if you can't do a
lot of research to pursue your critical viewpoint, you can
always quote passages from within the *one* text you are discussing. The personal response essay used for illustration
in Chapter 9, for example, quotes only from one source
(Didion's "On Going Home") to supply evidence.

Avoid Plagiarism

The word *plagiarism* means stealing somebody else's ideas
and passing them off as your own. It has its root in the
Latin *plagiarius*, meaning "kidnapper." Because a text is the
brain child of its author, you have no right to transport that
text into your own writing in such a way that you give the
impression it belongs to you. On the other hand, you do
have a right to quote or paraphrase someone else's work,
provided that you give credit to the author. Most plagiarism
results from failure to acknowledge sources properly.

Let's consider a situation in which plagiarism might occur. Suppose that you are writing a critical research essay on the Gettysburg Address. In the course of your research you find a book by D. E. Fehrenbacher about Lincoln, and within that book you come across this passage: "The heart of the matter for Lincoln, however, was the threat that secession posed to democratic government and its core principle, majority rule." Then let's say that you later write the following passage in your paper without acknowledging the source: "The heart of the matter for Lincoln was the threat that secession posed to democracy and to majority rule." If you write that, even though the words are not exactly the same as those of the original, you will have plagiarized. After all, you are taking an idea directly from Fehrenbacher's passage and restating that idea in almost the same terms. If your instructor finds out what you've done, you'll be in serious trouble.

However, you can still use Fehrenbacher's passage legitimately. All you have to do is make clear to your reader what you are doing. Consider the following passage, where credit is duly given:

> According to Fehrenbacher, "The heart of the matter for Lincoln . . . was the threat that secession posed to democratic government and its core principle, majority rule" (141).

Notice that the source is now acknowledged in three ways:

First, the phrase "According to Fehrenbacher, . . . " pinpoints the spot at which the source is being used. Lead-in phrases such as "According to" and "As so-and-so points out" are useful in marking an essay's areas of indebtedness and in distinguishing between the writer's viewpoint and that of a source.

Second, quotation marks surround the exact words that have been taken from the source. Although quotation marks are the standard means of showing that words are not your own, there is one other way to show that a passage is being quoted. In the case of a quote of five lines or longer, block

indentation can be used instead of quotation marks. The
blocked form (consistently indented 10 spaces from the left
margin) shows that the material is being quoted. (See the
examples on pages 126 and 127.)

Third, because the material is being quoted in a college
research paper, a parenthetical page citation follows the
quote. Term papers usually require page citings, even
though commercially published articles and books like this
one do not. From that citation the reader can assume that
the source of the quote will be found on page 141 of the
work by Fehrenbacher (the name given at the lead-in to the
quote) listed in a bibliography at the end of the student's
paper:

```
                    Works Cited
Fehrenbacher, Don E. Lincoln in Text and
    Context. Stanford: Stanford UP, 1987.
```

The form of the bibliography entry just shown follows MLA
style as described by Joseph Gibaldi and Walter S. Achtert
in the *MLA Handbook*, 3rd ed. (New York: Modern Language Association, 1988). MLA style is also introduced in
many college handbooks. You will probably need one of
those handbooks for guidance if you are doing a research
paper for an English course, since there are separate require-
ments for citing articles, multivolume works, reference
works, and so on. Besides MLA style there are several other
documentation formats in use across the disciplines, so that
you must be careful to check which is required in your
situation. What all formats have in common, however, is
the requirement that research papers cite fully the sources
being used.

Sometimes a source can be summarized or paraphrased
rather than quoted directly, but the need to acknowledge the
source remains. Here, for example, is a passage where material from Fehrenbacher's book is being briefly paraphrased
rather than quoted from directly:

Fehrenbacher has argued that the central issue for Lincoln

was the threat that Southern secession posed to democratic government (141–42).

Here again, a lead-in phrase ("Fehrenbacher has argued . . .") shows the reader where the indebtedness begins. This time, however, the words following that lead-in are a condensed paraphrase of the source rather than a word-for-word quotation. For that reason quotation marks or block indentation aren't used. But because the summarizing is taking place in a research paper, a parenthetical page-citation is again added to refer the reader to a bibliography listing at the back of the paper.

Students sometimes become confused about the need for source acknowledgments, since in theory all of our knowledge comes to us from outside sources. In general, if a specific fact or statistic can be looked up in five separate reference works, you needn't cite a source for it because it's considered "common knowledge." Thus, for example, you wouldn't have to acknowledge a source for stating that Lincoln's Gettysburg Address was delivered in 1863, even though you may have looked up that date in an encyclopedia. But once you've begun to borrow *interpretive* ideas, whether from an encyclopedia or from magazines, books, or other printed sources, you're dealing with material that should be acknowledged if you use it. Interpretive ideas include commentary or arguments made by other writers, factual information that isn't common knowledge, and of course any exact wording that you copy from a source.

Plagiarism results more often from ignorance of how to acknowledge sources than from deliberate intent. But occasionally the intent is there. A frustrated college student may feel overburdened by an assignment and try, in despair, to pass off someone else's essay as his or her own. That is sad, for it means the student has given up the will and opportunity to be a critical reader responding with a commentary of his or her own. Originality isn't hard if you have a critical point of view and if you respect your own thinking at least as much as you respect the ideas of others.

Quote Accurately

Closely related to the need for acknowledging sources is the need to represent them fairly. Unfair misrepresentation can occur in different ways, such as when you distort an author's argument or imply that the author's views are the same as those of someone whom he or she is summarizing. But the most common form of misrepresentation is the simple misquote.

Quoting accurately is not as easy as it seems. The human eye skips rather than sweeps along as it reads, so that it is possible to be looking straight at a word and not see every letter in it. This problem leads to inaccuracies not only in student papers but even in scholarly and commercial publishing. Also, because no one except the writer has time to check every quote against the original, chances are that any misquotation will go unrecognized by the reader unless it makes for a glaring error.

Types of misquotation include spelling slips, miscopied punctuation, lacunae (omissions), or accidental substitutions of phrasing. To see how all those kinds of error might come together in one unthinkable moment, consider the following passage:

> We need some imaginative simulus, some impossible deal which may shave vague rope and transform it into affective desire, to carry us gear after rear, without distrust, through the routing-work which is so large apart of life.

It would be an unpardonable sin to attribute that passage to Walter Pater, a Victorian author who wrote the following in his book *Marius the Epicurean* (1885):

> We need some imaginative stimulus, some not impossible ideal such as may shape vague hope, and transform it into effective desire, to carry us year after year, without disgust, through the routine-work which is so large a part of life.

Though it's unlikely that you or anyone else would misquote this passage as badly as in the previous example, even one or two of the slips shown could be enough to distort the author's meaning. Thus you should try hard to avoid any inaccuracy by double-checking every word and punctuation mark against the original text. And because it's possible that even the text you're quoting from may itself contain faulty transcribings from earlier editions, try always to do your quoting from the first or most scholarly edition available.

Do Not Draw Exaggerated Conclusions

After you've worked long and hard on a critical essay, there is always a temptation to draw an exaggerated conclusion when you reach the end. Because writing, like reading, is an act of discovery, you might feel a bit giddy when you feel you've uncovered some new truth about a text. But woe to the essayist who concludes a paper by writing something like this: " . . . I feel this book is without doubt the best of its kind and that its author will be considered great for many future generations and, indeed, for all time to come."

Like the sunset panorama at the end of a mediocre movie, this sort of ending implies more grandeur than it can deliver. First, it's unlikely that the critical essay will have proven that the book is the "best" (or "worst") of its kind, simply because the focus has been limited to the study of one or a few texts. Second, to predict what the future will hold for the reputation of *any* author is merely speculative. It would be much better simply to conclude the essay by summarizing the main points of analysis or by reaffirming a judgment in terms of the critic's own values. Rather than declaring something to be "the best" or "worst," consider stressing some social, emotional, rhetorical, logical, and/or ethical quality you have found it to have.

In *The Elements of Style*, William Strunk and E. B. White offer this warning: "Overstatement is one of the common faults. A single overstatement, wherever or however it occurs, diminishes the whole, and a single carefree superlative has the power to destroy, for the reader, the object of the writer's enthusiasm." Keep that warning in mind when you get to the last line of your essay.

Summary

Like reading, the act of writing is largely a process of discovery. There can be no iron rules about how to develop a critical essay. However, there are some guidelines that can help prevent confusion and guard against unpleasantness. Remember that you need to approach the text you're analyzing from a viewpoint of your own, possibly a viewpoint that personalizes one or more of the critical perspectives we've reviewed in this book. Remember, too, that discovering what you think about a text may call for some initial experiments, whether by posing questions, brainstorming, free writing, or other techniques. You should be prepared to cite the text for evidence that what you are saying about it is true. You should acknowledge whatever sources you use, quote accurately, and avoid drawing exaggerated conclusions. Those guidelines may not be all you need to know, but at least they will get you started.

A Glossary of Logical and Rhetorical Terms

Allusion.   Indirect reference to an event, a person, or another text. An example occurs at the beginning of the Gettysburg Address when Lincoln says, "Four score and seven years ago our fathers brought forth upon this continent, a new nation. . . . " The allusion is to the signing of the Declaration of Independence in 1776.

Ambiguity.   The quality of having two or more possible meanings. All language may be ambiguous to the extent that it can be interpreted differently by separate readers. But we may distinguish types of ambiguity according to their effects. For "good" ambiguity, see *symbol*. For "bad" ambiguity, see *mixed metaphor*.

Argument.   The giving of reasons to support an idea or belief. See also *deduction* and *induction*.

Argumentum ad baculum (appeal to force).   This is a fallacy implicit in a threat or an extortion. It is to be distinguished from a legitimate warning by the absence of any evidence — apart from the use of force — to show why a demand should be met:

> The Queen's argument was that, if something wasn't done about it in less than no time, she'd have everybody executed, all around.
>
> — Lewis Carroll

Argumentum ad hominem (attacking the person).   This is
a fallacy in which the writer attempts to discredit an
opponent's ideas by casting doubt on the opponent's
character. The reader is invited to replace logical
analysis with prejudice:

> No one would have suspected him to be a dishonest man,
> if he had not perversely chosen to assume a style which
> . . . the world always associates with dishonesty.

— Charles Kingsley

Argumentum ad populum (appeal to the crowd).   Known
as the "bandwagon fallacy," this kind of strategy appeals
to the reader's social or political sympathies in order to
win approval for a course of action. Peer pressure,
chauvinism, class identity, and other forms of collective
sentiment are the usual bases of assent. The bandwagon fallacy inspires blind faith in whatever a leader
says, rather than loyalty based on logic and fore-
thought:

> . . . you know how Caesar lov'd you.
> You are not wood, you are not stones, but men;
> And being men, hearing the will of Caesar,
> It will inflame you, it will make you mad.

— Marc Antony in
Shakespeare's *Julius Caesar* 3.2

Balanced sentence.   A formal sentence structure in which
the clauses rise and fall like the symmetry of a pyramid,
each side of the midpoint having approximately equal
length:

> If thine enemy be hungry, give him bread to eat; and if he
> be thirsty, give him water to drink[.]

— Proverbs 25.21

Classification/division.   This is a major rhetorical mode in
scientific texts. Classifying means grouping things according to like characteristics. Division means detecting
smaller classes within bigger ones. Effective classifica-

tion procedure depends on making the dividing basis for each new classification clear, so that the resulting subclasses do not overlap:

> If we confine our efforts to defining certain purely psychological types, the libidinal situation will have the first claim to serve as the basis of our classification.

> — Sigmund Freud

Comparison/contrast. This rhetorical mode calls attention to similarities and differences between two things. The writer shows how two subjects may be compared in some ways but contrasted in others:

> Man is only a reed, the weakest in nature; but he is a thinking reed.

> — Blaise Pascal

Deduction. A process of reasoning whereby conclusions are reached by the application of general categories to specific observations. For example: All people (general category) are mortal. Jane (specific observation) is a person. Therefore (conclusion) Jane is mortal. See also *enthymeme* and *syllogism*.

Definition. As a rhetorical mode, definition covers several techniques for explaining a term's meaning. A writer may define by means of a synonym (e.g., "Urticaria, also known as *hives*, is a common skin disorder"), by categorizing ("Cyclamen, a kind of tuberous perennial, is a popular ground cover"), or by quoting an authority ("Love," wrote George Chapman, "is Nature's second sun"). Another important means of definition is negation — saying what something is *not* in order to suggest what it is: "Progress," according to Herbert Spencer, "is not an accident."

Description. Although this word can be used loosely to mean giving details about something, it is more precisely understood to denote sense impressions — sight, sound, taste, touch, and/or scent. Description is often found in combination with narration in such forms as poetry, biography, history, the novel, and the personal essay:

> We would be tired at night and lie down in the accumulated heat of the little bedrooms after the long hot day and the breeze would stir almost imperceptibly outside and the smell of the swamp drift in through the rusty screens.

> —E. B. White

Diction. A writer's choice of words. The term "level of diction" is sometimes used to suggest how specialized the vocabulary of a text is. See also *jargon* and *verbosity*.

Either/or fallacy. This occurs when a text offers you only two choices when an issue may allow for three or more. Obviously, there are cases when events really must go in either of two ways (as when you flip a coin, for example). When Shakespeare's Hamlet asks "To be or not to be" the duality is legitimate because no third choice exists. But texts which try to simplify complex issues by artificially reducing a wide range of alternatives can slip into an either/or fallacy:

> Poets desire either to teach or to give pleasure.

> —Horace

Enthymeme. A deductive argument in which one of the basic premises is unstated. For example: "Mars is a planet in our solar system; therefore, it must revolve around the sun." Here, the unstated premise is that all planets in the solar system revolve around the sun. See *deduction*.

Equivocation. Writing or speaking with a deceptive intent. If someone writes "Nothing is too good for my neighbor," what sounds like a compliment may not be one.

Exposition. Writing whose main function is to expose and explain information. Works of nonfiction are usually expository texts.

Fallacy. An error in reasoning. We need not search far to encounter fallacies. They are all around us like insects in summer. Ordinary conversation is infested with them, and though serious texts are supposedly more scrupulous than talkers in how they express themselves, they too sometimes rely on absurd locutions just to get along. A fallacy is a way of jumping to a conclusion. The conclusion itself may be false or true, but if it is reached haphazardly the logic behind it will be dubious in either case. For examples of the more poisonous fallacies, see *argumentum ad baculum, argumentum ad hominem, either/or fallacy, hasty generalization, post hoc ergo propter hoc, question begging*, and *stereotyping*.

Fiction. A prose work about imaginary events. Subgenres of fiction include the novel, the romance, and the short story.

Figurative language. This term covers many kinds of non-literal expression found in both nonfiction and imaginative literature. See *metaphor, metonymy, personification, simile*, and *synecdoche*.

Form. A term denoting those aspects of a text which characterize its overall appearance. For example, a standard business letter's formal aspects may include an inside address, a salutation ("Dear . . . "), and a complimentary close such as "Sincerely." The form of a scholarly article may require footnotes or parenthetical citations, bibliography, as well as other features depending on the discipline. In drama and prose fiction, the arrangements of scenes and of dialogue may be regarded as formal components. The formal aspects of poetry are covered by the term *prosody*, which refers to such matters as rhyme scheme and stanza format.

Genre (French for "type"). The term refers to a major class or category of literature. Genres are usually classified on the basis of form rather than content. The broadest genre classifications are drama, poetry, fiction, and nonfiction. Each of those can be further subdivided according to the special forms occurring within it. Thus the short story is a subgenre of fiction, the essay is a subgenre of nonfiction, and so on.

Hasty generalization (converse accident). General statements are conclusions drawn from observation. Some general statements are less reliable than others, of course. The least reliable are those based on skimpy or misleading evidence. We call these *hasty* generalizations because they jump to conclusions about what truly characterizes a class of things or events:

> For the second time in our history, a British Prime Minister has returned from Germany bringing peace with honor. I believe it is peace for our time.
>
> — Neville Chamberlain

Hypothesis. A conclusion reached through inductive reasoning. Scientific experiments usually lead to hypotheses rather than to laws because future exceptions or new discoveries might invalidate present inference. See *induction*.

Illustration. The supplying of examples. Nonfictional writing is especially dependent on illustration to support what otherwise might seem vague or unearned generalizations. Sometimes an author will offer a long-extended example to illustrate a thesis (as Claude Levi-Strauss does in devoting an entire chapter of *Structural Anthropology* to the Oedipus myth in order to illustrate the principles of structuralism). Less formally, illustration shows up as multiple examples that bring general ideas into focus:

> The lives of Good Souls are crowded with Occasions, each with its own ritual which must be solemnly followed. On Mothers' Day, Good Souls conscientiously wear carnations; on St. Patrick's Day, they faithfully don boutonnieres of shamrocks; on Columbus Day, they carefully pin on miniature Italian flags. Every feast must be celebrated by the sending out of cards — Valentine's Day, Arbor Day, Groundhog Day, and all the other important festivals, each is duly observed.
>
> — Dorothy Parker

Induction. A process of reasoning whereby separate facts or data are brought together as evidence to support a hypothesis. Scientific conclusions that result from experiments are the product of inductive reasoning. See also *deduction*.

Irony. Wit, paradox, incongruity, or just saying one thing and meaning another — any of these can be an instance of irony. In general, literary critics regard irony as the holding of opposed ideas or emotions in balance. So-called "dramatic irony" occurs when the audience to a play knows that a character's fate is not going to be what the character on stage expects. In nonfiction, irony is present when the author takes emotional contrariety into account, balancing one extreme against another in a kind of paradox:

> . . . the lover demands a pledge, yet is irritated by a pledge. He wants to be loved by a freedom but demands that this freedom as freedom should no longer be free.
>
> — Jean-Paul Sartre

Jargon. Sometimes used to mean mere gibberish, the term should refer to specialized vocabulary used within a particular discipline. Jargon is an unfortunate but perhaps necessary part of higher education in many fields.

Logic. The science of reasoning. In general, logical analysis has to do with how conclusions are reached. See also *deduction*, *fallacy*, and *induction*.

Metaphor. A figure of speech that equates two unlike things:

> The moon was a ghostly galleon
>   tossed upon cloudy seas.
>
> — Alfred Noyes

Metonymy. The naming of an object to stand for a larger concept with which it is associated. For example: "They expect support from Capitol Hill."

Misplaced modifier. An instance of "bad" ambiguity caused by the position of a descriptive word or phrase. If your

Aunt Irma writes "We gave cupcakes to Susie's friends with pink frosting on them," the last phrase of the sentence is misplaced. Nevertheless, we are not likely to suppose that the friends were frosted. The problem is worse if your employer writes, "We all agreed Friday to meet for lunch, and I hope you'll make arrangements." (Did the agreement occur on Friday, or are you supposed to arrange for a Friday lunch?)

Mixed metaphor. A confused figure of speech. When a writer tries to express two or more imaginative comparisons in the same phrase, the result may be incoherent. For example, you would have a right to wonder what a politician meant by this: "We must launch ourselves into a new era of soaring prosperity and stop floating on economic quicksand."

Narration. Telling about events as they occur over time. As a rhetorical mode, narration is common in any type of text that must explain the past: novels, histories, personal memoirs, and so on. If a narrative is *chronological* it will follow a direct course from beginning to end. But if it is a so-called *dramatic narrative* it will begin in the middle of things, then allude to the beginning before proceeding to the end. A famous example of dramatic narrative is found in Charles Dickens's *A Christmas Carol*, where Scrooge's story moves from his later years back to his youth and then on to a vision of his future. Narrative writing is often accompanied by other rhetorical modes, especially description.

Nonfiction. As a genre, nonfiction is comprised of texts whose aim is to present factual as opposed to imaginary information. Major categories of nonfiction include autobiography, biography, the essay, history, and philosophy, as well as scientific and technical writing across the disciplines.

Parallelism. As an aspect of syntax, parallelism means expressing coordinate terms in similar form unless there is a good reason for doing otherwise. Why write "I like reading and to paint" when you could achieve parallel balance by writing "I like reading and painting"? Parallelism can also apply to other aspects of composition. Alliteration, for example, is a kind of audible parallelism that is especially important in poetry, where repeated sounds contribute to a sonorous effect ("O *Att*ic shape! Fair *att*itude" — John Keats). We can also find parallelism throughout the entire organization of a text. In many novels a subplot "parallels" the main plot. And it is not uncommon for an essay or nonfictional book to treat several subtopics at more or less parallel lengths.

Periodic sentence.   A sentence in which much of the predicate is placed before the grammatical subject:

> Of all the Affections which attend Human Life, the Love of Glory is the most Ardent.
>
> — Richard Steele

Personification.   The attributing of human characteristics to a nonhuman thing or idea:

> When the green woods laugh with the voice of joy
> And the dimpling stream runs laughing by . . .
>
> — William Blake

Post hoc ergo propter hoc.   The Latin means "after this therefore because of this" and alludes to the fallacy of assuming that an event can be explained on the basis of circumstantial evidence. Mystery books tease us with this fallacy by tricking us into suspicions that are later shown to be invalid. If a man is found murdered hours after an argument with his wife, it might seem reasonable to accuse the wife. But in fact it would not be reasonable without evidence showing motive, opportunity, and probable cause. Many people jump to conclusions about what causes accidents, crimes, diseases, wars, as well as events of good fortune. But a serious investigator recognizes that assigning a cause in the absence of conclusive evidence is a serious breach of logic:

> Since Senator X was elected, our state's economy has improved — we have him to thank!

> — *campaign rhetoric*

Process analysis. This rhetorical mode is concerned with explaining how something happens. If you are reading a text that falls into the "how-to" category — a diet or exercise guide, a popular book on how to overcome despair and achieve bliss, and so on — you will probably find a process being analyzed as a series of stages or steps. Technical manuals are dependent on process analysis, as are many books dealing with mathematics and other scientific skills. Occasionally, the mode also inhabits works of philosophy. In Oriental literature, for example, the great *Tao* analyzes the process of achieving full consciousness.

Question begging (*petitio principii*). This is a common fallacy in which the argument's main premise contains a conclusion which has yet to be proven. For example, "Outlawing credit cards is a good idea because without the cards people would save money." The statement offers no basis for assuming that money would be saved. If evidence were subsequently given, the assertion might be more persuasive, but predictive statements like this are often simply left to beg for the reader's approval. Another form of question begging is the so-called *circular argument*: "Product X is worth buying because of the reputation of its manufacturer; that reputation is deserved because of worthwhile products like X." Here again, the mark of a begged question is the absence of clear evidence to support the basic assertion.

Rhetoric. The art of using language in speaking and in writing. Among the ancient Greeks rhetoric meant techniques of persuasion. In modern education we use the term "rhetorical mode" to denote a way of presenting information, whether within single sentences or across whole paragraphs. For major rhetorical modes, see *classification/division*, *comparison/contrast*, *definition*, *description*, *illustration*, *narration*, *process analysis*, and *summary*.

Simile. A figure of speech in which a word such as *like* or *as* is used to make an imaginative comparison:

> My life is like a broken bowl, . . .
>
> —Christina Rossetti

Standard sentence. Also called "loose sentence," this form of syntax is common in English prose. The sentence begins with its grammatical subject, then adds a predicate which may contain any number of refinements:

> Books are the Legacies that a great Genius leaves to Mankind, which are delivered down from Generation to Generation, as Presents to the Posterity of those who are yet unborn.
>
> —Joseph Addison

Stereotyping. This term is now used to denote a fallacy of prejudice, whereby the reader is invited to accept without proof a notion that all members of a sex, race, nationality, religion, and so on, can be explained by one or a few common traits. Even when used poetically or humorously, it should be recognized as a dangerous oversimplification:

> Man's love is of man's life a thing apart;
> 'Tis woman's whole existence. . . .
>
> —a character speaking in Lord Byron's *Don Juan*

Summary. Though people often think of this rhetorical mode as a mere device for marking transitions (e.g., "Up to now we have dealt with zebras; now we shall turn to crocodiles"), it does have far greater strategic importance. As a means of distilling source information, it is an indispensable factor in scholarly texts

which must sum up background material or give a
quick review of matters indirectly related to the subject:

> Less than a hundred years after Copernicus, Kepler pub-
> lished (between 1609 and 1619) the three laws which de-
> scribe the paths of the planets. The work of Newton and
> with it most of our mechanics spring from these laws.

> —J. Bronowski

Syllogism.   An argument in which a conclusion is drawn
from the relation between two premises:

Major premise: All writers make mistakes.

Minor premise: Louise is a writer.

Conclusion: Louise makes mistakes.

A syllogism can be faulty if the minor premise does not
involve its subject in the first category established by
the major premise. For example, it would be false to
reason that because all writers make mistakes and
Louise makes mistakes that Louise is a writer—for
others besides writers can make mistakes, too. On the
other hand, a syllogism can proceed correctly but reach
a false conclusion if either of the premises can be disproved. For example: All writers are idealists; Louise is
a writer; therefore Louise is an idealist. (In this case,
the deductive logic is correct but the conclusion may
be false because the major premise is open to question.)
See also *enthymeme.*

Symbol.   A symbol is a visible image used to suggest an
abstract idea. In the Bible, for example, the rainbow
becomes a symbol of the Old Testament Covenant. In
the Gettysburg Address, the battlefield to which Lincoln refers becomes a symbol of devotion. But symbols
can also suggest more than one abstract idea at a
time, and for that reason they may embody "good" as
opposed to "bad" ambiguity. See also *ambiguity* and
description.

Synecdoche.   The naming of a part of something to represent the whole ("All hands on deck!") or of the whole

to stand for representative members ("Baltimore beat Cincinnati by a score of six to five").

Syntax. The arrangement of words, phrases, and clauses within sentences. See *balanced sentence, parallelism,* and *periodic sentence, standard sentence.*

Translation. A rendering from one language into another. Some translators try to give a "literal" (i.e., word-for-word) equivalence, while others try to translate the "sense" by freely substituting their own phrasing. Both ways of translating distort the original text, however slightly. A reader must therefore be careful about assuming that any translation is "accurate."

Trope. A figure of speech. See *figurative language.*

Verbosity. This term means "wordiness." More specifically, it refers to the habit of using two or more words where one would do. Such phrases as "the reason is because" (for *because*), "continue on" (for *continue*), and "at this particular point in time" (for *now*) are verbose. Careful editing is the most effective cure for this problem.

Bibliography

The following is a selected list of contemporary works related to the subject of critical reading. Because these works vary widely in audience level, I have tried to rate relative difficulty by means of asterisks. The span is from one asterisk (indicating easy reading for a general audience) up to five asterisks (indicating difficult reading even for an experienced scholar). This rating system is of course very subjective.

Adler, Mortimer J., and Charles Van Doren. *How to Read a Book*. Rev. ed. New York: Simon, 1972.*

Altick, Richard D. *Preface to Critical Reading*. 5th ed. New York: Holt, 1969.***

Barthes, Roland. *The Pleasure of the Text*. Trans. Richard Miller. New York: Noonday-Farrar, 1975.****

Bartholomae, David, and Anthony R. Petrosky. *Facts, Artifacts and Counterfacts*. Upper Montclair, NJ: Boynton/Cook, 1986.**

Bleich, David. *Subjective Criticism*. Baltimore: Johns Hopkins UP, 1978.***

Booth, Wayne C. *Critical Understanding*. Chicago: U of Chicago P, 1979.****

Cohen, Gillian. "The Psychology of Reading." *New Literary History* 4 (1972): 75–90.****

Copi, Irving M. *Introduction to Logic*. 5th ed. New York: Macmillan, 1978.***

Derrida, Jacques. *Of Grammatology*. Trans. Gayatri Spivak. Baltimore: Johns Hopkins UP, 1976. *****

Eco, Umberto. *The Role of the Reader*. Bloomington: Indiana UP, 1978. ****

Fetterly, Judith. *The Resisting Reader: A Feminist Approach to American Fiction*. Bloomington: Indiana UP, 1978. ****

Fish, Stanley. *Is There a Text in This Class?* Cambridge, MA: Harvard UP, 1980. ****

Gadamer, Hans-Georg. *Truth and Method*. London: Sheed, 1975. ****

Hayakawa, S. I. *Language in Thought and Action*. 3rd ed. New York: Harcourt, 1972. ***

Hirsch, E. D., Jr. *Cultural Literacy*. New York: Vintage-Random, 1988. **

Holland, Norman. *The Dynamics of Literary Response*. New York: Oxford UP, 1968. ****

Iser, Wolfgang. *The Act of Reading: A Theory of Aesthetic Response*. Baltimore: Johns Hopkins UP, 1978. ****

Miller, J. Hillis. *The Ethics of Reading*. New York: Columbia UP, 1987. ****

Nell, Victor. *Lost in a Book: The Psychology of Reading for Pleasure*. New Haven: Yale UP, 1988. ***

Ong, Walter J. "The Writer's Audience Is Always a Fiction." *PMLA* 90 (1975): 9–21. ***

Poulet, Georges. "Criticism and the Experience of Interiority." *The Structuralist Controversy*. Ed. Richard Macksey and Eugenio Donato. Baltimore: Johns Hopkins UP, 1972. 56–72. ***

Richards, I. A. *Principles of Literary Criticism*. 1924; rpt. ed. New York: Harcourt, 1959. ****

Said, Edward W. *The World, the Text, and the Critic*. Cambridge, MA: Harvard UP, 1983. ****

Smith, Barbara Herrnstein. *Contingencies of Value*. Cambridge, MA: Harvard UP, 1988. ****

Smith, Frank. *Understanding Reading: A Psycholinguistic Analysis of Reading and Learning to Read*. 3rd ed. New York: Holt, 1982. ***

Steiner, George. "'Critic'/'Reader'." *New Literary History* 10 (1979): 423–52. ****

Suleiman, Susan, and Inge Crosman, eds. *The Reader in the Text: Essays on Audience and Interpretation.* Princeton: Princeton UP, 1980.***

Tompkins, Jane P., ed. *Reader-Response Criticism.* Baltimore: Johns Hopkins UP, 1980.****

Appendix

The three texts included in this appendix are discussed widely in Parts II and III of this book. As part of your practice in developing critical reading skills, you may wish to continue discussing these texts on your own or with other readers.

The Gettysburg Address

Abraham Lincoln

Abraham Lincoln (1809–1865) was the sixteenth president of the United States. The following address was delivered on November 19, 1863, at Gettysburg, Pennsylvania. Lincoln had been invited to speak at the dedication of a national cemetery honoring Civil War soldiers who had fought at Gettysburg in July of that year. There are several hand-written copies of the speech which vary slightly in wording and punctuation. The text below is based on the copy known as the Everett manuscript.

Four score and seven years ago our fathers brought forth upon this continent, a new nation, conceived in Liberty, and dedicated to the proposition that all men are created equal.

Now we are engaged in a great civil war, testing whether that nation, or any nation so conceived, and so dedicated, can long endure. We are met on a great battle-field of that war. We have come to dedicate a portion of that field, as a final resting place for those who here gave their lives, that that nation might live. It is altogether fitting and proper that we should do this.

But, in a larger sense, we can not dedicate — we can not consecrate — we can not hallow — this ground. The brave men, living and dead, who struggled here, have consecrated it, far above our poor power to add or detract. The world will little note, nor long remember, what we say here, but it can never forget what they did here. It is for us, the living, rather, to be dedicated here to the unfinished work which they who fought here, have, thus far, so nobly advanced. It is rather for us to be here dedicated to the great task remaining before us — that from these honored dead we take increased devotion to that cause for which they here gave the last full measure of devotion — that we here highly resolve that these dead shall not have died in vain — that this nation, under God, shall have a new birth of freedom — and that, government of the people, by the people, for the people, shall not perish from the earth.

On Going Home

Joan Didion

Joan Didion (b. 1934) is a contemporary essayist and novelist. She served as an editor of *Vogue* during the 1960s and has more recently worked as a free-lance writer. The following essay is from her first collection of essays, *Slouching Towards Bethlehem* (1968).

I am home for my daughter's first birthday. By "home" I do not mean the house in Los Angeles where my husband and I and the baby live, but the place where my family is, in the Central Valley of California. It is a vital although troublesome distinction. My husband likes my family but is uneasy in their house, because once there I fall into their ways, which are difficult, oblique, deliberately inarticulate, not my husband's ways. We live in dusty houses ("D-U-S-T," he once wrote with his finger on surfaces all over the house, but no one noticed it) filled with mementos quite without value to him (what could the Canton dessert plates mean to him? how could he have known about the assay scales, why should he care if he did know?), and we appear to talk exclusively about people we know who have been committed to mental hospitals, about people we know who have been booked on drunk-driving charges, and about property, particularly about property, land, price per acre and C-2 zoning and assessments and freeway access. My brother does not understand my husband's inability to perceive the advantage in the rather common real-estate transaction known as "sale-leaseback," and my husband in turn does not understand why so many of the people he hears about in my father's house have recently been committed to mental hospitals or booked on drunk-driving charges. Nor does he understand that when we talk about sale-leasebacks and right-of-way condemnations we are talking in code about the things we like best, the yellow fields and the cottonwoods and the rivers rising and falling and the mountain roads closing when the heavy snow comes in. We miss each other's points, have another drink and regard the fire. My brother refers to my husband, in his presence, as "Joan's husband." Marriage is the classic betrayal.

Or perhaps it is not any more. Sometimes I think that those of us who are now in our thirties were born into the last generation to carry the burden of "home," to find in family life the source of all tension and drama. I had by all objective accounts a "normal" and a "happy" family situation, and yet I was almost thirty years old before I could talk to my family on the telephone without crying after I had hung up. We did not fight. Nothing was wrong. And yet some nameless anxiety colored the emotional charges between me and the place that I came from. The question of whether or not you could go home again was a very real part of the sentimental and largely literary baggage with which we left home in the fifties; I suspect that it is irrelevant to the children born of the fragmentation after World War II. A few weeks ago in a San Francisco bar I saw a pretty young girl on crystal take off her clothes and dance for the cash prize in an "amateur-topless" contest. There was no particular sense of moment about this, none of the effect of romantic degradation, of "dark journey," for which my generation strived so assiduously. What sense could that girl possibly make of, say, *Long Day's Journey into Night?* Who is beside the point?

That I am trapped in this particular irrelevancy is never more apparent to me than when I am home. Paralyzed by the neurotic lassitude engendered by meeting one's

past at every turn, around every corner, inside every cupboard, I go aimlessly from room to room. I decide to
meet it head-on and clean out a drawer, and I spread the
contents on the bed. A bathing suit I wore the summer I
was seventeen. A letter of rejection from *The Nation*, an
aerial photograph of the site for a shopping center my
father did not build in 1954. Three teacups hand-painted
with cabbage roses and signed "E.M.," my grandmother's
initials. There is no final solution for letters of rejection
from *The Nation* and teacups hand-painted in 1900. Nor
is there any answer to snapshots of one's grandfather as a
young man on skis, surveying around Donner Pass in the
year 1910. I smooth out the snapshot and look into his
face, and do and do not see my own. I close the drawer,
and have another cup of coffee with my mother. We get
along very well, veterans of a guerrilla war we never
understood.

Days pass. I see no one. I come to dread my husband's
evening call, not only because he is full of news of what
by now seems to me our remote life in Los Angeles,
people he has seen, letters which require attention, but
because he asks what I have been doing, suggests uneasily
that I get out, drive to San Francisco or Berkeley. Instead
I drive across the river to a family graveyard. It has been
vandalized since my last visit and the monuments are
broken, overturned in the dry grass. Because I once saw
a rattlesnake in the grass I stay in the car and listen to a
country-and-Western station. Later I drive with my father
to a ranch he has in the foothills. The man who runs his
cattle on it asks us to the roundup, a week from Sunday,
and although I know that I will be in Los Angeles I say,
in the oblique way my family talks, that I will come.
Once home I mention the broken monuments in the
graveyard. My mother shrugs.

I go to visit my great-aunts. A few of them think now
that I am my cousin, or their daughter who died young.
We recall an anecdote about a relative last seen in 1948,
and they ask if I still like living in New York City. I have

lived in Los Angeles for three years, but I say that I do. The baby is offered a horehound drop, and I am slipped a dollar bill "to buy a treat." Questions trail off, answers are abandoned, the baby plays with the dust motes in a shaft of afternoon sun.

It is time for the baby's birthday party: a white cake, strawberry-marshmallow ice cream, a bottle of champagne saved from another party. In the evening, after she has gone to sleep, I kneel beside the crib and touch her face, where it is pressed against the slats, with mine. She is an open and trusting child, unprepared for and unaccustomed to the ambushes of family life, and perhaps it is just as well that I can offer her little of that life. I would like to give her more. I would like to promise her that she will grow up with a sense of her cousins and of rivers and of her great-grandmother's teacups, would like to pledge her a picnic on a river with fried chicken and her hair uncombed, would like to give her *home* for her birthday, but we live differently now and I can promise her nothing like that. I give her a xylophone and a sundress from Madeira, and promise to tell her a funny story.

1967

Making Science Work

Lewis Thomas

Lewis Thomas (b. 1913) is a New York physician and former president of the Sloan-Kettering Center for Cancer Research. His columns and articles for academic journals have been collected in a number of well-known books. The following piece is from *Late Night Thoughts on Listening to Mahler's Ninth Symphony* (1983).

For about three centuries we have been doing science, trying science out, using science for the construction of what we call modern civilization. Every dispensable item of contempory technology, from canal locks to dial telephones to penicillin to the Mars Lander, was pieced together from the analysis of data provided by one or another series of scientific experiments — also the technologies we fear the most for the threat they pose to civilization: radioactivity from the stored, stacked bombs or from leaking, flawed power plants, acid rain, pesticides, leached soil, depleted ozone, and increased carbon dioxide in the outer atmosphere.

Three hundred years seems a long time for testing a new approach to human interliving, long enough to settle back for critical appraisal of the scientific method, maybe even long enough to vote on whether to go on with it or not. There is an argument. Voices have been raised in protest since the beginning, rising in pitch and violence in the nineteenth century during the early stages of the industrial revolution, summoning urgent crowds into the streets any day these days on the issue of nuclear energy. Give it back, say some of the voices, it doesn't really work, we've tried it and it doesn't work, go back three hundred years and start again on something else less chancy for the race of man.

The scientists disagree, of course, partly out of occupational bias, but also from a different way of viewing the course and progress of science in the past fifty years. As they see it, science is just at its beginning. The principal discoveries in this century, taking all in all, are the glimpses of the depth of our ignorance about nature. Things that used to seem clear and rational, matters of absolute certainty — Newtonian mechanics, for example — have slipped through our fingers, and we are left with a new set of gigantic puzzles, cosmic uncertainties, ambiguities; some of the laws of physics are amended every few years, some are canceled outright, some undergo revised versions of legislative intent as if they were acts of Congress.

In biology, it is one stupefaction after another. Just thirty years ago we called it a biological revolution when the fantastic geometry of the DNA molecule was exposed to public view and the linear language of genetics was decoded. For a while things seemed simple and clear; the cell was a neat little machine, a mechanical device ready for taking to pieces and reassembling, like a tiny watch. But just in the last few years it has become almost imponderably complex, filled with strange parts whose functions are beyond today's imagining. DNA is itself no longer a straightforward set of instructions on a tape. There are long strips of what seem nonsense in between the genes, edited out for the assembly of proteins but essential nonetheless for the process of assembly; some genes are called jumping genes, moving from one segment of DNA to another, rearranging the messages, achieving instantly a degree of variability that we once thought would require eons of evolution. The cell membrane is no longer a simple skin for the cell; it is a fluid mosaic, a sea of essential mobile signals, an organ in itself. Cells communicate with one another, exchange messages like bees in a hive, regulate one another. Genes are switched on, switched off, by molecules from the outside whose nature is a mystery; somewhere inside are switches which, when thrown one way or the other, can transform any normal cell into a cancer cell, and sometimes back again.

It is not just that there is more to do, there is everything to do. Biological science, with medicine bobbing somewhere in its wake, is under way, but only just under way. What lies ahead, or what *can* lie ahead if the efforts in basic research are continued, is much more than the conquest of human disease or the amplification of agricultural technology or the cultivation of nutrients in the sea. As we learn more about the fundamental processes of living things in general we will learn more about ourselves, including perhaps the ways in which our brains, unmatched by any other neural structures on the planet, achieve the earth's awareness of itself. It may be too much to say that we will become wise through such endeavors, but we can at least come into possession of a level of information upon which a new kind of wisdom might be based. At the moment we are an ignorant species, flummoxed by the puzzles of who we are, where we came from, and what we are for. It is a gamble to bet on science for moving ahead, but it is, in my view, the only game in town.

The near views in our instruments of the dead soil of Mars, the bizarre rings of Saturn, and the strange surfaces of Saturn, Jupiter, Venus, and the rest, literally unearthly, are only brief glances at what is ahead for mankind in the exploration of our own solar system. In theory, there is no reason why human beings cannot make the same journeys in person, or out beyond into the galaxy.

We will solve our energy problems by the use of science, and in no other way. The sun is there, to be sure, ready for tapping, but we cannot sit back in the lounges of political lobbies and make guesses and wishes; it will take years, probably many years, of research. Meanwhile, there are other possibilities needing deeper exploration. Nuclear fission power, for all its present disadvantages, including where on earth to put the waste, can be made safer and more reliable by better research, while hydrogen fusion, inexhaustibly fueled from the oceans and much safer than fission, lies somewhere ahead. We may learn to produce vast amounts of hydrogen itself, alcohol or methane, when we have learned more about the changeable genes of single-celled microorganisms. If we are to continue to burn coal in large amounts, we will need research models for predicting how much more carbon dioxide we can inject into the planet's atmosphere before we run into the danger of melting the ice shelves of western Antarctica and flooding all our coasts. We will need science to protect us against ourselves.

It has become the fashion to express fear of computers — the machines will do our thinking, quicker and better than human thought, construct and replicate themselves, take over and eventually replace us — that sort of thing. I confess to apprehensions of my own, but I have a hunch that those are on my mind because I do not know enough about computers. Nor, perhaps, does anyone yet, not even the computer scientists themselves. For my comfort, I know for sure only one thing about the computer networks now being meshed together like interconnected ganglia around the earth: what they contain on their microchips are bits of information put there by human minds; perhaps they will do something like thinking on their own, but it will still be a cousin of human thought once removed and, because of newness, potentially of immense usefulness.

The relatively new term "earth science" is itself an encouragement. It is nice to know that our own dear planet has become an object of as much obsessive interest to large bodies of professional researchers as a living cell, and almost as approachable for discovering the details of how it works. Satellites scrutinize it all day and night, recording the patterns of its clouds, the temperatures at all parts of its surface, the distribution and condition of its forests, crops, waterways, cities, and barren places. Seismologists and geologists have already surprised themselves over and over again, probing the movement of crustal plates afloat on something or other, maybe methane, deep below the surface, meditating the evidences now coming in for the reality and continuing of continental drift, and calculating with increasing precision the data that describe the mechanisms involved in earthquakes. Their instruments are becoming as neat and informative as medicine's CAT scanners; the earth has deep secrets still, but they are there for penetrating.

The astronomers have long since become physicists, the physicists are astronomers; both are, as well, what we used to call chemists, examining the levels of ammonia or formaldehyde in clouds drifting billions of light-years away, measuring the concentrations of methane in the nearby atmosphere of Pluto, running into paradoxes. Contemporary physics lives off paradox. Niels Bohr said that a great truth is one for which the opposite is also a great truth. There are not so many neutrinos coming from our sun as there ought to be; something has gone wrong, not with the sun but with our knowledge. There are radioastronomical instruments for listening to the left-over sounds of the creation of the universe; the astronomers are dumbstruck, they can hardly hear themselves think.

The social scientists have a long way to go to catch up, but they may be up to the most scientific business of all, if and when they finally get down to the right questions. Our behavior toward each other is the strangest, most unpredictable, and almost entirely unaccountable of all the phenomena with which we are obliged to live. In all of nature there is nothing so threatening to humanity as humanity itself. We need, for this most worrying of puzzles, the brightest and youngest of our most agile minds, capable of dreaming up ideas not dreamed before, ready to carry the imagination to great depths and, I should hope, handy with big computers but skeptical about long questionnaires and big numbers.

Fundamental science did not become a national endeavor in this country until the time of World War II, when it was pointed out by some influential and sagacious advisers to the government that whatever we needed for the technology of warfare could be achieved only after the laying of a solid foundation of basic research. During the Eisenhower administration a formal mechanism was created in the White House for the explicit purpose of furnishing scientific advice to the President, the President's Science Advisory Committee (PSAC), chaired by a new administration officer, the Science Adviser. The National Institutes of Health, which had existed before the war as a relatively small set of laboratories for research on cancer and infectious disease, expanded rapidly in the postwar period to encompass all disciplines of biomedical science. The National Science Foundation was organized specifically for the sponsorship of basic science. Each of the federal departments and agencies developed its own research capacity, relevant to its mission; the programs of largest scale were those in defense, agriculture, space, and atomic energy.

Most of the country's basic research has been carried out by the universities, which have as a result become increasingly dependent on the federal government for their sustenance, even their existence, to a degree now causing alarm signals from the whole academic community. The ever-rising costs of doing modern science, especially the prices of today's sophisticated and complex instruments, combined with the federal efforts to reduce all expenditures, are placing the universities in deep trouble. Meanwhile, the philanthropic foundations, which were the principal source of funds for university research before the war, are no longer capable of more than a minor contribution to science.

Besides the government's own national laboratories and the academic institutions there is a third resource for the country's scientific enterprise — industry. Up to very recently, industrial research has been conducted in relative isolation, unconnected with the other two. There are signs that this is beginning to change, and the change should be a source of encouragement for the future. Some of the corporations responsible for high technology, especially those involved in energy, have formed solid linkages with a few research universities — MIT and Cal Tech, for example — and are investing substantial sums in long-range research in physics and chemistry. Several pharmaceutical companies have been investing in fundamental biomedical research in association with medical schools and private research institutions.

There needs to be much more of this kind of partnership. The nation's future may well depend on whether we can set up within the private sector a new system for collaborative research. Although there are some promising partnership ventures now in operation, they are few in number; within industry the tendency remains to concentrate on applied research and development, excluding any consideration of basic science. The academic community tends, for its part, to stay out of fields closely related to the development of new products. Each side maintains adversarial and largely bogus images of the other, money-makers on one side and impractical academics on the other. Meanwhile, our competitors in Europe and Japan have long since found effective ways to link industrial research to government and academic science, and they may be outclassing this country before long. In some fields, most conspicuously the devising and production of new scientific instruments, they have already moved to the front.

There are obvious difficulties in the behavior of the traditional worlds of research in the United States. Corporate research is obliged by its nature to concentrate on

profitable products and to maintain a high degree of se-
crecy during the process; academic science, by its nature,
must be carried out in the open and depends for its progress on the free exchange of new information almost at
the moment of finding. But these are not impossible barriers to collaboration. Industry already has a life-or-death
stake in what will emerge from basic research in the years
ahead; there can be no more prudent investment for the
corporate world, and the immediate benefit for any cor-
poration in simply having the "first look" at a piece of
basic science would be benefit enough in the long run.
The university science community, for all the talk of
ivory towers, hankers day and night for its work to turn
out useful; a close working connection with industrial researchers might well lead to an earlier perception of po-
tential applicability than is now the case.

The age of science did not really begin three hundred
years ago. That was simply the time when it was realized
that human curiosity about the world represented a deep
wish, perhaps embedded somewhere in the chromosomes
of human beings, to learn more about nature by experiment and the confirmation of experiment. The doing of
science on a scale appropriate to the problems at hand
was launched only in the twentieth century and has been
moving into high gear only within the last fifty years. We
have not lacked explanations at any time in our recorded
history, but now we must live and think with the new
habit of requiring reproducible observations and solid
facts for the explanations. It is not as easy a time for us
as it used to be: we are raised through childhood in skepticism and disbelief; we feel the need of proofs all
around, even for matters as deep as the working of our
own consciousness, where there is as yet no clear prospect of proof about anything. Uncertainty, disillusion,
and despair are prices to be paid for living in an age of
science. Illumination is the product sought, but it comes
in small bits, only from time to time, not ever in broad,

bright flashes of public comprehension, and there can be
no promise that we will ever emerge from the great
depths of the mystery of being.

Nevertheless, we have started to do science on a world
scale, and to rely on it, and hope for it. Not just the
scientists, everyone, and not for the hope of illumination,
but for the sure predictable prospect of new technologies,
which have always come along, like spray in the wake of
science. We need better ways of predicting how a piece
of new technology is likely to turn out, better measures
available on an international level to shut off the ones
that carry hazard to the life of the planet (including, but
perhaps not always so much *first of all*, as is usually the
only consideration, our own species' life). We will have
to go more warily with technology in the future, for the
demands will be increasing and the stakes will be very
high. Instead of coping, or trying to cope, with the wants
of four billion people, we will very soon be facing the
needs, probably desperate, of double that number and,
soon thereafter, double again. The real challenge to
human ingenuity, and to science, lies in the century to
come.

I cannot guess at the things we will need to know from
science to get through the time ahead, but I am willing
to make one prediction about the method: we will not be
able to call the shots in advance. We cannot say to ourselves, we need this or that sort of technology, therefore
we should be doing this or that sort of science. It does
not work that way. We will have to rely, as we have in
the past, on science in general, and on basic, undifferentiated science at that, for the new insights that will open
up the new opportunities for technological development.
Science is useful, indispensable sometimes, but whenever
it moves forward it does so by producing a surprise; you
cannot specify the surprise you'd like. Technology should
be watched closely, monitored, criticized, even voted in
or out by the electorate, but science itself must be given
its head if we want it to work.

The following pages of acknowledgments constitute a continuation of the copyright page.

Page 10: From *Webster's New World Dictionary*, Third College Edition, © 1988. Reprinted by permission of the publisher, Webster's New World Dictionaries/A Division of Simon & Schuster, Inc., New York, New York 10023.

Page 14: Excerpt from "What I Believe" in *Two Cheers For Democracy*, copyright 1939 and renewed 1967 by E.M. Forster, reprinted by permission of Harcourt Brace Jovanovich, Inc.

Page 18: From Maya Angelou, *I Know Why The Caged Bird Sings*. Copyright © 1969 by Maya Angelou. Reprinted by permission of Random House, Inc.

Pages 18–19; 87–88: Excerpts from *A Brief History of Time* by Stephen W. Hawking, copyright © 1988 by Stephen W. Hawking, Interior Illustrations copyright © 1988 by Ron Miller. Used by permission of Bantam Books, a division of Bantam, Doubleday, Dell Publishing Group, Inc.

Page 19: From Woody Allen, "My Speech to the Graduates," Op-ed page, *The New York Times* 10 August 1979. Copyright © 1979 by The New York Times Company. Reprinted by permission.

Page 20: From Ernest Hemingway, *A Moveable Feast*. Copyright © 1964 by Ernest Hemingway Ltd. Published by Charles Scribner's Sons, a division of Macmillan, Inc.

Page 20: From *The Right Stuff* by Tom Wolfe. Copyright © 1979 by Tom Wolfe. Reprinted by permission of Farrar, Straus & Giroux, Inc.

Page 22: From Maxine Hong Kingston, *The Woman Warrior: Memoirs of a Girlhood Among Ghosts*. Copyright © 1976 by Maxine Hong Kingston. Reprinted by permission of Alfred A Knopf Inc.

Pages 22–23: From Jonathan Schell, *The Fate of the Earth*. Copyright © 1982 by Jonathan Schell. Reprinted by permission of Alfred A Knopf Inc.

Page 48 and *passim*: From William Strunk, Jr., and E.B. White, *The Elements of Style*, 3rd edition. Copyright © 1979 by Macmillan Publishing Co., Inc.

Page 76: From Roy P. Basler, "Abraham Lincoln's Rhetoric," *American Literature* 11 (1939): 167–82. Reprinted by permission of Duke University Press.

Pages 78–79: From Carl Sandburg, "Abraham Lincoln: The Soil and the Seed" in *Literary History of the United States*, edited by Robert E. Spiller et al. 4th edition. Vol. 1. Copyright © 1974 by The Macmillan Company.

Pages 79–80: Excerpt from "Abraham Lincoln" from *Patriotic Gore* by Edmund Wilson. Copyright © 1962 by Edmund Wilson. Originally published in *The New Yorker* 14 March 1953. Reprinted by permission of Farrar, Straus & Giroux, Inc.

Pages 84–85: From Barbara W. Tuchman, *The Guns of August*. Copyright © 1962 by Barbara W. Tuchman. Published by The Macmillan Company.

Page 86: From Larry J. Goldstein, David C. Lay, and David I. Schneider, *Calculus and Its Applications*, 5th edition. Copyright © 1990 by Prentice-Hall, Inc. Reprinted by permission of the publisher.

Page 89: From Frederic S. Mishkin, *The Economics of Money, Banking, and Financial Markets*, 2nd edition. Copyright © 1989 by Mishkin Economics, Inc. Reprinted by permission of Scott, Foresman and Company.

Page 91: From H.W. Janson, *History of Art*, 3rd edition. Englewood Cliffs, NJ:

Prentice-Hall, Inc.; New York: Harry N. Abrams, Inc., 1986. Reprinted by permission of Harry N. Abrams, Inc.

Page 93: From Helen Vendler, *The Music of What Happens*. Copyright © 1988 by the President and Fellows of Harvard College. Reprinted by permission of Harvard University Press.

Page 108: From Roland Barthes, *The Pleasure of the Text*, trans. Richard Miller. Noonday-Farrar translation copyright © 1975 by Farrar, Straus & Giroux, Inc. Reprinted by permission of the publisher.

Page 118: From Susan Brownmiller, *Femininity*. Copyright © 1984 by Susan Brownmiller. Published by Linden Press, a division of Simon & Schuster, and under the Fawcett Columbine imprint of Ballantine Books, a division of Random House, Inc. Reprinted by permission of Simon and Schuster, Inc.

Page 125: From Martin Washburn, Review of *The Lives of a Cell*, by Lewis Thomas, *The Village Voice* 27 June 1974: 32–33. Reprinted by permission of the author, Martin Washburn.

Page 127: From Jonathan Yardley, "Lewis Thomas: A Doctor of Humane Letters," *The Washington Post Book World* 13 November 1983: 3 + . Copyright © 1983 The Washington Post. Reprinted by permission.

Pages 127, 130: From Joyce Carol Oates, "Beyond Common Sense," *The New York Times* 26 May 1974: 2–3. Copyright © 1974 by The New York Times Company. Reprinted by permission.

Pages 137–138: From Denis Donoghue, "The Young Yeats," *The New York Review of Books* 14 August 1986. Reprinted with permission from *The New York Review of Books*. Copyright ©1986 Nyrev, Inc.

Page 139: From Don E. Fehrenbacher, *Lincoln in Text and Context*. Copyright © 1987 by the Board of Trustees of the Leland Stanford Junior University. Reprinted by permission of Stanford University Press.

Page 147: From Sigmund Freud, "Libidinal Types," *International Journal of Psycho-Analysis* 13 (1932): 277–80. Reprinted by permission.

Page 148: From E.B. White, *Essays of E.B. White*. Copyright © 1977 by E.B. White. Reprinted by permission of Harper & Row, Publishers, Inc.

Page 150: From Dorothy Parker, "Good Souls," *Vanity Fair* June 1919. Courtesy *Vanity Fair*. Copyright © 1919 (renewed 1947) by The Condé Nast Publications Inc.

Page 151: From Jean-Paul Sartre, *Being and Nothingness*, trans. Hazel E. Barnes. Copyright © 1956 by the Philosophical Library, Inc. Reprinted by permission of the publisher.

Page 151: From Alfred Noyes, "The Highwayman," *Collected Poems*. Copyright © 1947 Alfred Noyes. Reprinted by Permission of Harper & Row, Publishers, Inc.

Page 156: From J. Bronowski, *Science and Human Values*, revised edition. Copyright © 1965 by J. Bronowski. Reprinted by permission of Harper & Row, Publishers, Inc.

Pages 166–169 and *passim*: "On Going Home" from *Slouching Towards Bethlehem* by Joan Didion. Copyright © 1967, 1968 by Joan Didion. Reprinted by permission of Farrar, Straus & Giroux, Inc.

Pages 170–178 and *passim*: From *Late Night Thoughts on Listening to Mahler's Ninth Symphony* by Lewis Thomas. Copyright © 1981, 1982 by Lewis Thomas. Reprinted by permission of Viking Penguin, a division of Penguin Books USA Inc.

Index